STAR TREK™
BEYOND
THE MAKEUP ARTISTRY OF JOEL HARLOW

STAR TREK BEYOND
THE MAKEUP ARTISTRY OF JOEL HARLOW

ISBN: 9781785655876

Published by Titan Books
A division of Titan Publishing Group Ltd.
144 Southwark St.
London
SE1 0UP

First edition: October 2017

10 9 8 7 6 5 4 3 2 1

To receive advance information, news, competitions, and exclusive offers online,
please sign up for the Titan newsletter on our website: www.titanbooks.com

Did you enjoy this book? We love to hear from our readers.
Please e-mail us at: readerfeedback@titanemail.com or write to Reader
Feedback at the above address.

A CIP catalogue record for this title is available from the British Library.

Printed and bound in Canada.

Joel: To my family; Cindy, Jackie, Alec, Ashley, Bobby, Steve, Irene, Charlie and Peggy.
Joe: To 'Deacon' Joe Nazzaro, the original and still, by far, the best.

STAR TREK™
BEYOND
THE MAKEUP ARTISTRY OF JOEL HARLOW

CONTENTS

GOING ABOVE AND BEYOND

BY JUSTIN LIN

"STAR TREK SAYS THAT IT HAS NOT ALL HAPPENED, IT HAS NOT ALL BEEN DISCOVERED, THAT TOMORROW CAN BE AS CHALLENGING AND ADVENTUROUS AS ANY TIME MAN HAS EVER LIVED."
Gene Roddenberry

When I was probably 8 or 9 my family owned a small fish and chips restaurant in Orange County. We had emigrated from Taiwan and my parents had poured their life savings—and all of their waking hours—into making this restaurant a success in order to give us kids a shot at pursuing our dreams. My parents, brothers, and I were the restaurant's sole employees, so that meant we were usually there until 10pm every night (we only took Thanksgiving off). Our only solace on those long days was the promise of coming home and, after the evening news, watching reruns of *Star Trek* together as a family.

I like to think that's how most people of my generation discovered *Star Trek*: sitting in their living rooms with mom and dad, watching Kirk and Spock explore the universe, defeat the odd Klingon, and occasionally seduce a green alien lady (I made sure we had an Orion girl in *Beyond*). So, naturally, the first people I called were my parents when I was offered the chance to direct the next *Star Trek* movie. The excitement in their voices was all the encouragement I needed.

When I first came onto the then untitled *Star Trek 3* in January of 2015, we were in dire straits. We had no script, no crew, and needed to be shooting in six months. Our incredible writers (Doug Jung and Simon Pegg) immediately began toiling away night and day, and our production team scrambled to get the very best crew on board. After all, this film was to be the capstone of the 50th anniversary of *Star Trek*! So, when it came time to hire a makeup designer, only one name came up: Joel Harlow.

Joel is the type of makeup designer that needs no introduction. A casual glance at his IMDB page will tell you that he has worked on just about every movie worth seeing in the last 30 years. I mean, he already had an Academy Award for Makeup for *Star Trek* (2009)! However, when I met Joel for the first time, it wasn't his impressive resume or his Academy Award that won me over. It was his unbridled enthusiasm for what he does.

We talked for hours. You'd think he would have gotten it all out of his system, having already done a *Star Trek* movie, but no—he was just getting warmed up. He

"EACH TIME I SAID 'MORE', I COULD SEE JOEL'S EYES LIGHT UP. HE DIDN'T SEE IT AS BEING BURDENED WITH MORE WORK. INSTEAD, HE SAW IT AS IF WALLS WERE BEING TORN DOWN, AN OPPORTUNITY TO CREATE EVEN MORE."

Justin Lin on stoking Joel Harlow's creative fire

had sketchbooks, reference images, and some quick Photoshop mashups of ideas he wanted to try. I hired him on the spot.

It was around this time that we were really figuring out what *Star Trek 3* was going to be about. All I could think about was a family, say roughly 30 years from now, sitting down together to watch this film. Would they feel the same amount of wonder that I did watching 30 years ago? It became incredibly apparent to me that this movie could only go one place: beyond.

Now, when I say 'beyond', I mean that in every aspect of this film. Kirk and his crew were going to be pushing the boundaries of the Federation, and we were going to be pushing the boundaries of technology and craftsmanship. And in no place would that be more apparent than in the creation of Federation Starbase Yorktown. Every race in the galaxy bustling about in the very embodiment of Starfleet principles in one space station. While our production designer, Tom Sanders, and his team began designing what it would look like, it became Joel's job to populate it.

Joel and I would have in-depth discussions about their biologies: What types of creatures were they descended from? Do they breathe oxygen? If not, how would we incorporate that into their design? What do they sound like? How do they move?

Meeting after meeting, Joel came with new ideas. 'More' became my common mantra: "Bring me more aliens!" After all, this starbase was on the very frontier—it couldn't be just populated with aliens we had seen

before. Each time I said "more," I could see Joel's eyes light up. He didn't see it as being burdened with more work. Instead, he saw it as if walls were being torn down, an opportunity to create even more. Eventually, Joel proposed an idea: 50 aliens for 50 years. What better way to celebrate the 50th anniversary? (I think we actually ended up at 56).

This is all not even mentioning the myriad of iterations we went through in designing the looks of our villain, Krall. Or the evolution of the striking visage that became Jaylah. And Joel's job hardly ended there—if anything, it had just begun. Joel and his team not only designed all of our aliens, but also sculpted, created latex forms, painted, applied, and worked with our performers to make those designs come alive. Countless times did I arrive on set to find Joel and his crew, who had already been there since 3am, in full spirits, excited to show off the latest finished product.

In this book, you will get a glimpse of what I got to experience while working with Joel Harlow, Richie Alonzo, and all of their amazing team. The tireless and joyful creativity that brought to life the multitude of creatures you saw on screen in *Star Trek Beyond*. The same creativity that inspired me some 30 years ago in our family's tiny living room. I can only hope this book is the first of many that commemorate our collaborations together.

JUSTIN LIN
Director, *Star Trek Beyond*

A GALAXY OF POSSIBILITIES

BY SIMON PEGG

"Infinite diversity in infinite combinations."This was the concise manifesto and doggedly optimistic vision of the future, pitched to America's NBC television network in the mid 1960s by a certain producer and writer from El Paso, Texas, by the name of Eugene Wesley Roddenberry. *Star Trek* was to be a weekly science-fiction series about adventure and exploration, set at a time when the human race had learned to overcome its petty divisions and branch out into a bustling cosmos, *to boldly go where no man has gone before*. Of course, it became so much more.

Roddenberry imagined the Milky Way as a metropolitan expanse, crowded with a vast array of life forms ranging from familiar humanoids, murderous cyborgs and glowing blobs to sentient ribbons of pure energy and thought. In the intervening years, as the magnitude of space/time has become more apparent to us, the idea of our brief blue blip on the galactic radar coinciding with other civilisations at a similar developmental stage seems increasingly unlikely. In truth, though, the cold, hard realities of our place in the universe are no more relevant now than they were then.

Star Trek is the very essence of science fiction; a projection of our future, mirroring the hopes, fears and preoccupations of the present. Twenty-one years after the end of World War II, the show compounded the conservative optimism of the 1950s with permissive attitudes of the ensuing decade to create an aspirational future for the planet Earth. It took our small corner of space and turned it into a galaxy of possibilities. Yes, there were adversaries and challenges, but humanity faced them together, in collaboration with new friends and allies. A federation of worlds, determined to bring unity and peace to an ever-expanding frontier.

As a projection of the future, the original *Star Trek* was resonant of America's past, not least its colonial guilt. If Roddenberry's creation was indeed a 'Wagon Train to the Stars', this was a more benevolent journey into the west. The pioneers of Starfleet were far less invasive and destructive than their forbears. They were empathetic and sensitive towards the cultures they encountered, extending a hand of community and friendship, perpetuating and embracing diversity rather than relentlessly usurping, as colonisation inevitably

entails. It's easy to underestimate the psychological function of popular entertainment, particularly genre fare, which is often dismissed as benign fantasy. Yet every expression of human creativity reflects its epoch to some extent, and *Star Trek* was so much deeper than its minimal production values implied. This was cathartic soul searching at its most earnest, a vision of the human race putting right the wrongs that comprise its violent, troubled history. Roddenberry's audacious vision of a truly multicultural spaceship and an even more multicultural galaxy was a love letter to humanity, in spite of its shortcomings. It passionately insisted that maybe, just maybe, we could put things right.

Early in the writing process for *Star Trek Beyond*, Doug Jung and myself decided to put a physical embodiment of Gene Roddenberry's dream at the very heart of the story. Starbase Yorktown was an opportunity for us to demonstrate the Federation in action: a highly sophisticated hub at the edge of known space, where newly inducted Federation planets could gather on

neutral ground and get to know each other. As the screenplay puts it:

EXT. SPACE - NIGHT

The Enterprise *traveling on impulse power. As it comes about, we see its destination: YORKTOWN BASE. A massive FEDERATION STAR BASE on the edge of charted space. Built in conjunction with dozens of different alien Federation species. A nexus for all the nearby worlds that have been inducted into the Federation. Yorktown is large enough to house the millions of residents, visitors and workers who have just moved in. An idyllic multicultural hub invested with the spirit of everything the Federation stands for.*

This short passage was pretty much all we gave special FX makeup designer Joel Harlow and his team to go on before they set about creating the extraordinary variety of species aboard Yorktown. Descriptions of the villain Krall, ingenue heroine Jaylah, and mysterious alien foes

Manas and Kalara were similarly vague and brief, as were mentions of the non-human members of Starfleet. And yet Joel and his team took these minimal descriptions and created physical magic. Beings of every shape and size that never failed to thrill me both as a creative collaborator and a science-fiction fan. Every day I would step onto set and witness a new wonder emerging from the SPFX makeup trailer, a hive of activity that was always busy long before most of the cast and crew had even woken up.

Joel went so far as to create a different alien species for every year *Star Trek* has been part of the cultural consciousness. In doing so he presented the most thorough and effective rendering of Gene Roddenberry's super-inclusive galaxy that has ever been seen. I'd often find myself getting frustrated on set that a particularly exotic-looking creature would be positioned in the deep background, when surely it deserved a loving close-up and at least a minute of screen time. And yet this was intrinsically part of Joel's vision—infinite diversity

in infinite combinations, or at least the illusion of it. By conceiving a rich palette of alien diversity and having it just glimpsed, sometimes barely, that all-important sense of endless galactic variety pervades. In 1966, Eugene Wesley Roddenberry could only imagine the potential of his nascent creation; 50 years later, the award-winning team behind *Star Trek Beyond* have delivered on his promise.

Here then is the chance to savour the extraordinary work of Joel Harlow and his team. Fifty different makeups and models created for *Star Trek Beyond*, one for every year this tenacious and beloved story has been in our world. This plucky little TV show, which became not only the embodiment of inclusivity but also the champion of a philosophical direction we must surely strive for… to boldly go.

Live long and prosper.

SIMON PEGG, 2017

CHAPTER 1

LIFE BEFORE BEYOND

rowing up, I was very much a *Star Trek* fan. My family lived in Grand Forks, North Dakota, and I would watch the original TV series when we went to visit my grandparents in Denver, Colorado for Christmas and summer vacations. My cousin was an avid *Star Trek* fan at the time, and while I wasn't as devoted as he was, I've definitely become more of a fan as the years have gone by.

My first major influence in film and television was actually the original 1933 *King Kong*. I had seen it with my father one Thanksgiving and immediately knew I wanted to do something in this business; I just didn't know what it was because I was still quite young at the time. I just knew I wanted to do something that afforded me the ability to create magical characters like the one I was seeing on television.

As I got a little older, I began to figure out ways of creating movie magic. I started playing around with stop-motion and cell animation as a child, but after seeing *An American Werewolf In London* and *The Thing*, I realized what I was really interested in was special makeup and makeup effects. I ultimately went to the School of Visual Arts in New York, majoring in animation since they had an animation program, and makeup effects classes were hard to find.

The problem was at the time I was attending the School of Visual Arts, which was in 1986, there really weren't any schools for makeup. Dick Smith was running his mail-order advanced course, and there were a couple of weekend courses that Dean Kartalas was

offering through the Actor's Makeup Studio just off Times Square, so I enrolled in that while attending the School of Visual Arts. That's when I knew with complete certainty that this was what I wanted to do for a living.

Right around that time a friend of mine, Mark Pederson, had met a low-budget filmmaker in Florida named Tim Ritter, so in the summer of 1987 I went out there to work on my first movie: a low-budget horror film called *Killing Spree*. I was tasked with 'killing' seven people and bringing them back to life, all for just $1,000. Mark (who was also acting as cinematographer on the film) and I built everything in his parent's garage down in Tequesta, Florida.

After that first special makeup film experience I went back to New York, which is where I met Vincent Guastini. I ended up helping him on weekends working on *The Deadly Spawn 2: Metamorphosis*, sculpting the giant Deadly Spawn creature. Vincent was working on a devil character for *Toxic Avenger II* (which eventually became *Toxic Avenger II* and *III*), and passed it over to me to finish and apply, so I journeyed up to Peekskill, New York—I was actually still sculpting that makeup in the back of the van on the way!—and then molded it, ran the foam and built the wings, horns and teeth in an abandoned Masonic lodge that served as our lab/housing. It was absolutely a 'paying your dues' film experience. The only upside was getting to meet and work with people like David Grasso, Tim Considine, Jerry Macaluso and Roy Knyrim. It was a horrible experience for everyone involved, but we all stuck it through. After

"WORKING AT STEVE'S WAS AN AMAZING EXPERIENCE FOR AN
ARTIST BECAUSE HE CONTINUALLY THOUGHT OUTSIDE THE BOX."

Joel on being inspired by Steve Johnson at XFX

ABOVE (LEFT TO RIGHT): Airbrushing final Kalara makeup; double-teaming Manas makeup with Lennie MacDonald; touching up Ashley Edner as Natalia; Vulcan-eared makeup application.

we finished, I moved back home to Grand Folks and got a few menial jobs there while trying to figure out my next step.

I eventually returned to New York because my friend Mark was there now, and that's when I met Gabe Bartalos, joining his crew on *Basket Case 2*. When that was over, I went out to Los Angeles, which is where you had to be in the late eighties if you wanted to do makeup effects. Gabe had a job on a film that was shooting in Yugoslavia and was ultimately named *Happy Hell Night*. Dan Rebert and I built all the body parts for it in Gabe's studio in Sylmar, and Gabe and I traveled with them over to the location in Yugoslavia for filming. When I returned, I began shopping my slowly growing portfolio around, which led to me landing a job working at Steve Johnson's XFX. I wound up calling XFX home for about eight years, working on such projects as *The Stand, The Shining, Species, Virus, Lord of Illusions, Night of the Demons 2* and *The Shining* (the 1997 miniseries).

Working at Steve's was an amazing experience for an artist because he continually thought outside the box. There was never an A, B and C route to anything; makeup effects were always approached with an attitude of, 'How can we make it different?' This was in the late eighties and early nineties, before computer effects, so we did a lot of testing that now would be instantly relegated to the arena of digital effects. During this 'golden age', however, it was plastic-bag creatures, methylcellulose, silk organza, cotton candy, flash paper; anything that gave us an interesting look.

Some of the work I witnessed and participated in during my career at XFX was some of the most magical work I've ever seen, even though a lot of it never ended up on film. There were artists like Lennie MacDonald (who I brought with me on *Star Trek Beyond*), Bill Corso, Bill Bryan, Dave Dupuis, Nori Honda, Jim Kagel; it was a pretty amazing place to work. A lot of those folks were incredible, outside-the-box thinkers, Bill Bryan and Lennie being two of the biggest. Steve also had Leon Laderach, who was amazing at coming up with working, practical effects. We would do all these amazing video tests for various projects that were coming in. That kind of innovation doesn't exist anymore because it's too easy to relegate moments like transformations, elaborate character suits and makeups, and on-screen changes, to digital.

"I WAS WORKING WITH 45 OF HOLLYWOOD'S TOP MAKEUP ARTISTS... ALL I WANTED TO DO WAS WALK UP AND DOWN THE ROWS OF STATIONS AND WATCH OTHER ARTISTS' TECHNIQUES."

Joel on his extraordinary learning experience while working on The Grinch

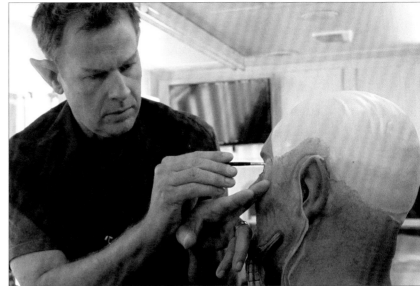

One of the major turning points in my career was when I got into IATSE (International Alliance of Theatrical Stage Employees). It opened up a whole new world for me because I was now applying makeups, whereas before I was sculpting them and only applying them if they were for a non-union project. Being in the union allowed me to hop around between projects, picking up new tricks and techniques from many incredible artists.

Working on *The Grinch*, for example, was a particularly amazing experience because I was working in a room with 45 of Hollywood's top makeup artists. When I would finish my makeup, all I wanted to do was walk up and down the rows of stations and watch other artists' techniques. Working in that environment under Rick Baker (who won an Oscar for the film) and Toni G was like a dream come true. That was my first union film, so I learned a lot. I already had a skill set I'd picked up at Steve Johnson's, but I also picked up a lot on *The Grinch* that helped me become the artist I am today.

While I was on *The Grinch* I met Ve Neill, who was about to do *A.I. Artificial Intelligence*. Prior to this, Bill Corso had been Ve's key makeup artist, but Bill was going off to department-head something else so Ve asked him for a recommendation—and he recommended me. Ve knew I came from a shop background, and as there were some accessory background characters that Stan Winston's shop was not building, I built them.

After *A.I.* the first *Pirates of the Caribbean* came up; Ve was asked to department-head and I came on as her key. Captive Audience was building what minimal prosthetics there were in the film, but when *Pirates of the Caribbean 2* and *3* came up, she campaigned to get the build for that film. I handled it for her with a group of artists I had met along the way. Prior to *Pirates*, I had done the creature work on *Buffy The Vampire Slayer* for half a season, as well as building characters for a few other television shows. It wasn't until *Pirates of the Caribbean 2* and *3*, however, where I was building and applying characters—and none more complicated and satisfying than the Bootstrap Bill character.

After that, I was asked by Johnny Depp to do *Alice in Wonderland* with Patty York (one of his makeup artists, Ve being the other one). The first *Star Trek* came after *Pirates of the Caribbean 3*, and that's when Barney Burman asked me to come in and work in the shop, and be his liaison to set…

CHAPTER 2

ENTERING THE
FINAL FRONTIER

When I was brought in to the *Star Trek* shop it was still quite early in pre-production, and a lot of decisions still had to be made. We still needed to create a variety of as yet undesigned characters. Neville Page had done some brilliant designs for a number of sequences in the film. Some of the aliens he had done, however, were not designed as makeups so we had a crack at translating some of those ideas into characters that could be done in a practical way with the use of prosthetics. Prior to that, the sculpting department was basically Don Lanning and I just trying to create some unusual and interesting alien races that could be placed in the background of different shots.

During those early days, there were no rules; we were just trying to come up with something unique to show our director, J.J. Abrams, with the hope of getting them okayed or at least getting feedback on the direction of what we were going to do. In addition to our runaway imaginations we drew upon references from the original TV show, and some of our favorite alien races. The idea was to potentially take some of those aliens and update them; Don did a really nice take on the Gorn and an updated Salt Vampire. Aside from that, we were just trying to come up with some interesting ways to distort the human body and head. We played around with using a combination of green screen and sculptural elements to create interesting alien anatomy.

There was one character in particular that I came up with, which was intended as a background mask. The look was basically two faces fused together; I utilized the actor's own eyes, with a face on either side that met in the middle. Barney Burman took that design and did a makeup version of it that ended up in the outtakes of the Klingon prison sequence.

I also did another version of the Talosians from the *Star Trek* pilot, which were originally women in makeup, using their own smaller proportions in contrast to giant heads with pulsating veins on them. What I did was sculpt an exaggerated head on a tiny neck; assuming it was approved, the performer's own neck would be green-screened out so the overall image would be a character with an oversized head on an unnaturally small alien neck.

As far as other alien races went, we knew the Vulcans were going to be in the film. We had already started work on the ears; in fact, I think I sculpted the very first version of what wound up being six separate test sculptures of Leonard Nimoy's ears in Barney's shop. We also knew the Romulans were coming, but since they started much later in the shooting schedule, they still hadn't been addressed at that point. In the meantime, we were still trying to populate the *Star Trek* universe, so the background alien characters were our immediate focus.

It eventually became obvious that there was already so much to do in this respect and the Romulans hadn't even been designed yet. It was at that point that producers Tommy Harper and Jeffrey Chernov, who knew I ran the shop on *Pirates of the Caribbean 2* and *3*, asked me to take over the primary alien races, those being the Vulcans, the Romulans and the Klingons.

I knew Barney was still going to be doing all the background characters, so I agreed with the understanding that I got to bring in my own people. I brought in the artists I worked with on the *Pirates of the Caribbean* films, including Steve Buscaino as my makeup lab supervisor. At that point it became Harlow Designs handling the Romulans, Vulcans and Klingons, although the Klingon sequence was cut from the final film.

Our Vulcans were pretty similar to the aesthetic that had come before, so there wasn't a lot of redesigning needed for them other than producing our prosthetic ears in silicone rather than foam. J.J. wanted the Romulans to be completely different, however. They still resembled Vulcans in terms of the pointed ears and eyebrow elements, but we went through half a dozen full makeup tests to determine the Romulan aesthetic, specifically for the character of Nero, played by Eric Bana. My contribution was the structural anatomy of the head, nose and brow, while Neville came up with different scarification patterns, tattoo patterns and piercing patterns. We ran the gamut on the modern primitive, coming up with dozens of different ideas based on that look. We also incorporated interesting hair patterns and ornamentation for some of the tests.

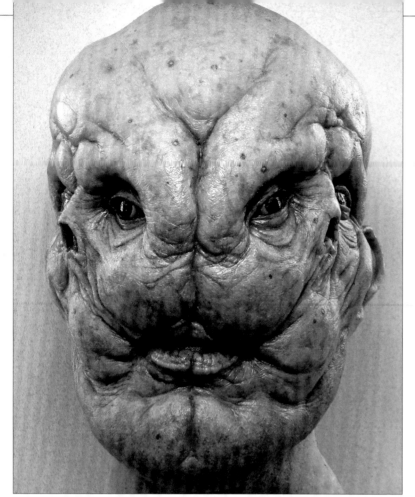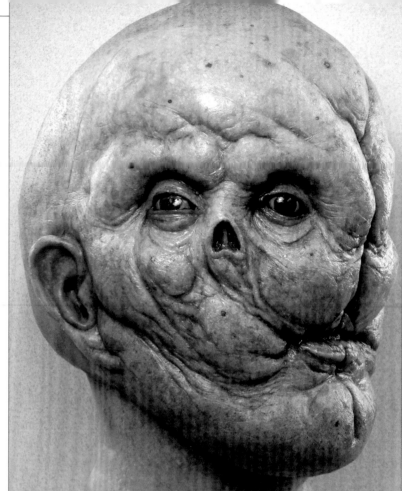

ABOVE: A three-faced background alien Harlow created for *Star Trek*, which used the actor's own eyes for the center face.

For the character of Nero specifically, I designed a head scar into the makeup that chopped off the top of his right ear. At the beginning of the film his ear is intact, but after he's released from the Klingon prison facility he sports a big bite-mark scar starting at the middle of his head, traveling down toward the corner of his eye and back along his ear, which is now missing. The Nero makeup was the most extensive of the Romulan prosthetics, comprising four pieces in total.

The other Romulans each had a three-piece makeup, which consisted of two ears and a forehead piece that typically blended at the crown of the head. There was also a piece on the right arm of all of the Romulans that was a Klingon branding scar, signifying that this crew were all part of the same group when they were in the Klingon prison on Rura Penthe. As the look of the Romulans was more of a militant crew, it was decided to make them all bald. All of the Romulan actors agreed to shave their heads, which made it much easier for us in the trailer.

Each Romulan had his own set of tattoos, and with 30–35 Romulan characters, there were a lot of tattoos. Neville designed all the tattoos, and made sure they were different enough to be individual, but similar enough to be from the same culture.

At our busiest point, shooting the scenes involving the Romulan ship *Narada*, I had approximately 35 people working with me. Luckily for us, there weren't a lot of other films shooting at the time, so we were able to get some really talented artists who also knew how to do lab work. I structured the department so we would do our makeups in the morning and then roll over into sculpting, casting or molding to keep the machine going. I was extremely fortunate to get that group of artists because we were using silicone appliances, which were still fairly new at the time, but they all embraced the look and turned out some amazing makeups.

Our Klingons were really more of a tease in *Star Trek*, because you weren't supposed to see them all that well. They wore helmets throughout the entire Klingon planet

BELOW: The first makeup test for Nero, sculpted and applied by Harlow to Neville Page.

NEVILLE PAGE ON DESIGNING THE ROMULANS

I had established a relationship with J.J. Abrams through working with him on *Cloverfield*, so he was responsible for bringing me in on *Star Trek* as creature designer. There were a couple of scenes with monsters that he wanted me to do, and when the Romulans became a hot topic he asked me to get involved with those too.

J.J. and I discussed what a Romulan would feel like, so we talked about scarification as a way of evolving that V-shaped forehead. When you see them in the original series they're human looking with pointy ears, but after many years they start to have that forehead shape, so my rationale was keyloid scarring over many years.

We also discussed the possibility of tattooing the face, which J.J. warmed up to. There was a hierarchy, so the hero had to be the boss, and from there the 'language' would trickle down to the various ranks. I must have done a hundred variations of that design so that each Romulan had his own distinct tattoo. It was an interesting challenge.

The problem was, there have been so many great tattoos over time, so my approach was like Russian prison tattoos: I figured these guys were such rogues that they would be tattooing one another, as opposed to going to a tattoo parlor. They'd be doing it on their ship or while in prison; things like that. And then I realized it's a specific band of Romulans, so you had to dig a little deeper into their aesthetic. It's like the Hell's Angels have a totally different set of tattoos than, say, a bunch of Hispanic gang-bangers. It meant thinking about the culture of the gang versus the culture of an entire race.

Ironically, I found myself in the movie because Joel did his first test on me. There was no budget to hire somebody for the tests so I said, 'I believe in this design, so I'll come in early and shave my head for this, so do whatever you need to!' Joel needed to prove some things to convince Eric Bana to go down that path, so it was fantastic to sit in the chair while he was exploring and experimenting.

ABOVE: Harlow working on one of *Star Trek*'s never-seen Klingons.

ABOVE: David Dupuis airbrushes a Romulan extra.

scene, so you never saw their full faces. All you really saw was the area around their eyes and mouth. I sculpted and cast a facial appliance that was basically like a Lone Ranger piece that fit around their eyes. We punched hair into that, which gave it the effect of being a Klingon without having to build an entire makeup. The helmets helped convey the traditional Klingon bone structure. Since you would only see the skin area around their eyes, the helmets helped sell the fact that they were Klingons.

I can't remember when I first heard about possible Oscar consideration for the film, but I know I wasn't able to make it to the 'bake-off' (which is where artists from the shortlisted films discuss their work and show a clip from it), but Barney and Mindy Hall, our makeup department head, were able to represent our work there. I was in Venice with Johnny Depp on *The Tourist* at the time when I heard we were nominated—I couldn't believe it. It was all very new to me; not that it's old hat now, but I was certainly less experienced in the whole award campaign season than I am now. So it all came out of left field. Looking back, I was just going along for the ride, and I think Mindy did all the heavy lifting as far as speaking and campaigning.

When *Star Trek Into Darkness* came up a few years later, Tommy Harper approached me about working on it, but I had to turn it down due to the fact that I was already committed to doing *The Lone Ranger*. I was in Boston with Johnny on *Black Mass* when my friend Jeffrey Chernov contacted me about *Star Trek Beyond*. After working on the first *Star Trek* film and missing out on the second, I knew I wanted to do this one. I also knew *Pirates of the Caribbean 5* was coming up, so I was gutted that they were happening simultaneously.

I went to Johnny and got his blessing to go and tackle *Beyond*. He told me at the beginning of our partnership that if there was ever a movie I really wanted to do, I should feel free let him know and go do it. He is an artist firstly, so he knows when a passion project comes along, you need to seize it. I owe a great deal to Johnny in addition to calling him a friend, so it was bittersweet to temporarily leave his company for this opportunity. So that's what happened. I said, 'Look, there's this new *Star Trek* film coming up and I really want to do it, because it's got the potential for a lot of interesting characters'. I made sure Johnny was in good hands for *Pirates 5* and that's how I came aboard *Star Trek Beyond*...

ABOVE: Mike Smithson touches up a Romulan extra.

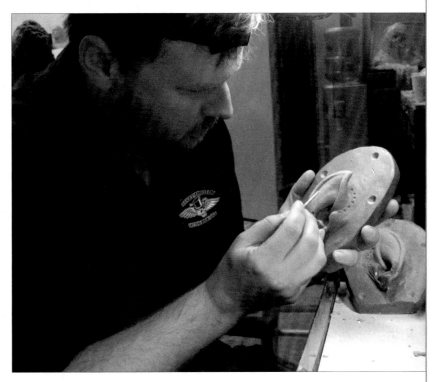

ABOVE: Harlow finishes detailing a set of Spock ears for initial test.

CHAPTER 3

BEGINNING BEYOND

The thing that interested me most about *Star Trek Beyond* was the potential opportunity to do something nobody had ever done before in the *Star Trek* universe. The nature of the story lent itself to creating a boundless number of alien races that didn't have a pre-established aesthetic we would have to follow. That was exciting! We could explore new and radical aesthetics, yet we were very conscious that we were working in the *Star Trek* universe. We didn't want to deviate too much from the classic *Star Trek* alien feeling, but there was certainly a way to update them and make them believable for a film in 2016.

I had close to 70 different artists helping me bring everything together, consisting of a massive crew in Burbank, which is where we started prep, another large crew when we moved up to Vancouver to start shooting, and finally a more scaled-down crew when we finished shooting in Dubai. It's important to note that every one of those people contributed to the look of the film and the work in this book. If you took away any one of them, the work would not have been what it is today.

Although I approved everything, I encouraged everybody to bring their own ideas to the table. That's why I bring in the top people in the business. The sculptors I brought in, such as Joey Orosco, Norman Cabrera, Matt Rose, Don Lanning, Miles Teves and Richie Alonzo, are instantly sucked up by other studios as soon as they finish a project, but we were lucky to start work at a time when there wasn't a lot happening so I was really fortunate to get these guys. Every time I locked in another key artist I thought, 'I can't believe I got them!'

There's something about working on a *Star Trek* film that is quite appealing for people of my generation, and a lot of the artists on this combined crew of 70-something people were *Star Trek* fans. I think there was also an added enthusiasm based on the success of the last two films, and what J.J. Abrams did in rebooting the whole franchise. I can't tell you how many people came up to me and said, 'This is the best time I've had working in a shop!' It reminded me of working in the shops in the eighties, when it was a bunch of monster makers, creature makers and character makers just having a good time creating. That's the kind of vibe that we had throughout the whole project... rare these days.

As far as concept designers, I brought in Carlos Huante and Allen Williams, who are both brilliant illustrators. I've been a fan of their work for a long time, and was really lucky to get them. They rendered some great concept illustrations for me from the very beginning, when we weren't exactly sure what we were going for. The way it came together was after I met our director, Justin Lin, there was a period of time when we knew we needed aliens for one sequence or another, but weren't sure if they were going to stay in that scene or move to

another. That gave us a lot of freedom, so everybody was throwing out ideas. Ultimately, I would say 75% of those alien characters made it into the film in one form or another.

As the story and the size of the film started to grow, we needed to populate some areas with new races. We would go back to some of our previous illustrations and present them to Justin, who would make notes and changes. By the end of the process, he had enough confidence in us to pretty much let us create whatever we wanted, knowing that we wouldn't deliver him anything that wasn't worthy of his film. Carte blanche to create alien character makeups—is there anything better?

In the beginning we played around with the idea of bringing back some of the classic, pre-established *Star Trek* aliens, but I thought that would have been counterproductive to what we were trying to do, which was to expand this universe. What we were trying to do was give the fans a whole palette of characters, faces and races.

One of the things that makes an alien fit into the *Star Trek* aesthetic is that it's a makeup. No matter how big or augmented that character is, it's still an actor performing through a makeup. All of us on the film are makeup artists, and that's our passion. We want to accomplish transformations rather than apply tracking markers or pop a mask on them. There were certainly a

"MY BIGGEST PRIORITY FROM THE START WAS TO MAKE EVERY CHARACTER LOOK AS GOOD AS WE COULD POSSIBLY MAKE IT."

Joel on his approach to Star Trek Beyond

ABOVE: Norman Cabrera surrounded by his sculpting work on *Star Trek Beyond*.

ABOVE: Erin Peters painting up a set of alien arms for Reptilicus.

few, but I would say 75% of the characters we created were makeups. *Star Trek* brings out the kid in all of us, so all of our actors were really excited about playing an alien in a *Star Trek* film as well.

Our two main alien characters were Krall, played by Idris Elba, and Jaylah, played by Sofia Boutella. Krall undergoes a transformation throughout the film, so his character has four different stages of makeup, from a very extreme look to a more humanoid appearance.

Our biggest challenge from day one was finding out, through design and sculpture, what Krall looked like. Sometimes you can over-focus on a character to the point that you overdesign all the 'magic' out of it. Since Krall's look was so important to get right, we spent a lot of creative energy on him, scrutinizing every shape and wrinkle. We were reworking and second-guessing right up to the last couple weeks before we shot. That was scary because it was potentially disastrous if we didn't pull it off, and we weren't about to settle for 'good enough' when we were shooting for 'great'. Since everyone was a professional and excited about that challenge, we accomplished our goal, basically redoing Krall's makeup just a week and a half out from shooting.

Neville Page had a team of artists working on the film just as we did, which is where the Jaylah design came from, brilliantly translated by Richie Alonzo. There were a lot of different versions at first, but the one we ultimately went with was the one that resonated with everybody, and I don't think we deviated from that final look at all. The real challenge became a matter of getting those lines to look crisp and precise, and how we integrated her skin tone into the hair color. It was a matter of refining all of those elements; the aesthetic was already there.

My biggest priority from the start was to make every character look as good as we could possibly make it. I didn't want to be sitting in the theater when the film came out thinking, 'If I had only stayed up another three hours, it would have looked even better!' Fortunately, nobody required convincing of that; we were all on the same page.

NEVILLE PAGE (CONCEPT ARTIST): I was brought in at the beginning when Bob Orci was director, so we started developing things, and then the production shut down and picked up again with a new director. That was

"THERE WAS THIS WONDERFUL COMPETITIVE SPIRIT, AND BECAUSE JOEL AND I HAD A HISTORY TOGETHER, WE WOULD INSPIRE EACH OTHER IN TERMS OF OUR TEAMS' EFFORTS."

Concept artist Neville Page on bringing the best out of the Star Trek Beyond creatives

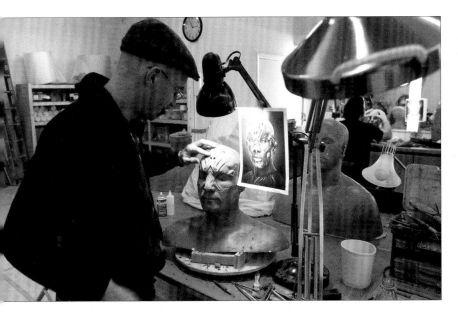

ABOVE: John Wrightson checking unused sculpture against original concept design.

ABOVE: Marc Opdycke sculpting another set of alien arms.

an interesting situation because we started with a ton of designs, but there was no script the second time around because it was a whole re-start. At that point we were just designing 'Bad Guy.' There was no real description of him because they were still trying to figure out what the parameters were going to be. It was a fascinating way of starting work on a character, because most of us like to know what it is we're doing. There was an idea that this character kept changing and morphing all the time, but that could be anything. Is he morphing from human to butterfly? Is there a cocoon change? So at the beginning it was just broad strokes, let's just design some bad guys.

We also had Jaylah, so we knew we had a bad guy and a good girl to design, but nobody cast as actors. Idris was not even on the radar—at least not ours—so we started designing on generic heads because we knew they had to be practical makeups. There were a couple of characters that were going to be full CG, but after you become experienced with these types of shows, you realize that it's not so much aimless as much as in development and you're all discovering it together, so that can be kind of fun if you're in the right state of mind.

I was brought in to generally address all the topics, but the most important ones were, 'What does the Idris character look like, and what does the good girl Jaylah look like?' I was brought in as primary concept designer on the outside, while Joel was brought in as makeup designer, so I had a small team and he had his small team. But it was very clear to both of us that we were going to be working quite closely together at the beginning to make sure we were on the same mission, even though we were bringing new and different ideas to the table.

What was interesting is there was this wonderful competitive spirit, and because Joel and I had a history together, we would inspire each other in terms of our teams' efforts. There were times when Joel's team would do something that kicked our butts, and sometimes we did something that inspired Joel's team. That was really cool, because he had his vision as far as how he was art-directing and perceiving the narrative, and I had mine, so in the end we had a really broad range of ideas.

And because I was friends with a lot of his artists, it was pretty much one giant resource of incredible talent, generating ideas that ranged from traditional sculpting

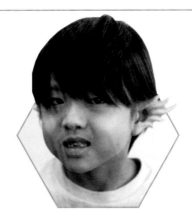

to pencil drawings; we were all over the map in terms of how we approached it.

In the end, there was no one person who achieved the final look of the Krall character. I've always used the analogy that it's like a relay race: someone ends up carrying the baton to the finish line and that was Joel, but Joel was only able to bring it to the finish line because of the other people running like mad around the course as well. There's rarely been a project where one person is responsible for the whole thing—it's always about the collaborative effort, and the evolution of the various inspirations.

RICHIE ALONZO (SCULPTOR / MAKEUP ARTIST):

It was towards mid-December when I knew they were having problems with the script, so they shut down during Christmas break, and we heard they were starting up again in January with a totally new script and a new director. We went in and read the new script and it was totally different. It didn't have Nimoy or Shatner in it, and there was this new character, Krall, but the script was a real page-turner with a lot of action and a big battle in which the *Enterprise* gets destroyed.

There was a new alien nemesis, and so much more to do in terms of makeups and alien characters, so we were really jazzed about that. We got started immediately, setting up a shop in Burbank and sculpting makeups

from the designs that had been approved, so that was the beginning.

The original version of Krall was going to be a combination of makeup and live effects. The character supposedly had energy coursing through his body, so you could see light traveling up into his head and stuff like that. We did some tests for the scenes in which Krall goes through his transformations where he's absorbing energy, and Lennie MacDonald came up with some really amazing ideas, but I don't think any of it ever saw the light of day. We showed them to the producers as a possible jumping-off point, but they never really came to fruition.

It wasn't until we started in January that we heard Idris Elba was going to play Krall, so that was pretty exciting because he's such a dynamic actor. We were really excited about the idea of seeing him in the makeup and seeing what he could do with it.

ALLEN WILLIAMS (CONCEPT ARTIST): I've been
a huge *Star Trek* fan since I was a kid, from the original series on up, so there was no way Joel could have presented this project to me that I would have turned it down. Basically what he said was, 'We're doing this movie in the *Star Trek* universe, and we've got a lot of free rein to play around with it'. The only thing I had to keep in mind at all times was whereas other movies completely build things through CG, *Star Trek* tends to focus more on

makeup and practical effects that can be built onto human characters. So that was the only thing to keep in mind; that these things still had to be built and worn on the human body.

For me, the initial decision is much more fluid and fast if I'm sitting down with a pencil and just playing around with graphite. Once I get past that, everything else is just a matter of what I can use to produce the most functional piece of work for the art director or production manager to look at. I would usually start and finish things with graphite, and if they liked those designs, I would then scan them and proceed to render and tweak, and sometimes leap into Z-Brush and produce a maquette.

I worked on the film for about three months, and actually felt more at home when we got closer to the end of it because I had really settled into this nice groove of creativity. To me, it's always strange to talk about film work because it's such a collaborative effort, you get used to the fact that 'we' did this. But Joel was one of the best art directors I've ever worked with in terms of pushing you in the right direction.

CARLOS HUANTE (CONCEPT ARTIST): Joel sent me an email, and we started talking about the film. Our original designs for the bad guy were not for a specific actor, but at some point when we thought it was going to be Bryan Cranston, I thought, 'Great, he's got a good-looking bone structure you can design around!' But when you look at that face, you don't want a lot of rubber on him because he's going to be acting a lot, so all of those things have to be taken into account. So I was thinking about how little rubber to put on this guy's face yet still make him look interesting. I would like to have spent a lot more time on that, but that went away and we went from no actor to Bryan Cranston, and then Idris Elba.

I actually wanted to redesign some of the old *Star Trek* characters, so I think I did a Ferengi and an Andorian, but we didn't follow up with any of those ideas. I really liked the original Andorian look, and the first version of the Ferengi was really interesting, before they got commercialized for *Deep Space Nine*. So it would have been fun to do something with them.

Looking back, I really liked working with Joel, and meeting some of the other guys and learning there are

ABOVE: Vancouver painters Erin Peters, Caitlin Groves and Bronwyne Sloley.

ABOVE: Tracy Lai (foreground) and Toby Lindala (background) in the Vancouver lab.

"AS SCULPTORS AND DESIGNERS, JOEL AND I WERE BOTH ABLE TO GET JUSTIN VERY EXCITED ABOUT THE POTENTIAL OF THESE [MAQUETTES]."

Designer and sculptor Don Lanning on impressing director Justin Lin

still people out there who care about this stuff enough to put themselves into it. That makes me feel very good about the future of what we're doing. I loved working on *Star Trek Beyond*. The original 1960s show is still one of my favorites so this was a big deal for me, and I'm really glad I got to work on it.

DON LANNING (DESIGNER/SCULPTOR): I believe I was the first phone call from Joel, which was the last quarter of 2014, and I believe we did maybe ten aliens, maybe more for that first incarnation of the film, including a couple of really bizarre creatures. Some of them were 'get out of here, we don't want that', including a very heavily tentacled alien that Bob Orci, the original director, liked that looked like it was going to get in at one point. And then there was some controversy about his script and over the Christmas holiday everything closed down.

In my own head I was worried, because it was *Star Trek* and I wanted to be part of it, so it was a difficult Christmas. Jump ahead several weeks and I got a call from Joel saying, 'We're back on!' We had a new

director, Justin Lin, and we had an outright rejection of anything that had gone before because it was a new script, so Joel told me to shelve everything we had done so far. That wasn't a big deal, because we had only done maybe 10 to 15 maquettes and some of them were pretty wild.

We had three of the top designers in the world: Neville Page, Carlos Huante and Allen Williams, while I was the practical guy in the room. And as we know, the practical guy is not necessarily the leader in that race, so there was a real John Henry aspect to it. Every time I did a maquette, I would purposely leave my tools and the remains of clay at the base of the sculpture. I would deliberately leave them in the photos that were delivered to Justin Lin. So the fact I was able to move two concepts a day in real clay and you could see the debris and the labor involved I think played a major role for Joel and I inasmuch as it was a treat within the meetings and conference calls to get to that real, tactile sculpture. As sculptors and designers, Joel and I were both able to get Justin very excited about the potential of these things.

ABOVE: Kevin Haney life-casts the ears of future Vulcan Cindy Harlow.

ABOVE: Daemon Cadman, part of the Vancouver painting team.

ALIEN CHARACTER GUIDE

JAYLAH | KRALL | MANAS | KALARA | ENSIGN SYL

KEENSER | T'VANA | ORION GIRL | JAE | STATIC

SPOCK | ZAVANKO | QUILLS | REPTILICUS | WADJET

J-9 | JIN | MERELL | MARTI | SATINE

KLINGONS | THE TEENAXI | NATALIA | ELEPHANT SLUG | VULCANS

KEY CHARACTERS | THE ENTERPRISE | ALTAMID

DEEP C-ZER · HUSKS · BOLTAAN · CLASSIC ALIEN · SHLERM

SHELDON · CRABBIE · SIR OLDEN · COCO · LOLEEKI

BROK · BARLOWE · AKIMA · SNAIL · JASKELL

BEZOS · RUSS · BOGGS · SHAZEER · THROG

JOSEPH · EGGHEAD · WILBUR · PESCA · ALA

THE TEENAXI · YORKTOWN

CHAPTER 4

THE ALIENS OF
STAR TREK BEYOND

What was different about this film compared to some of the others I've done is that Justin Lin, J.J. Abrams, Simon Pegg, Doug Jung, Lindsey Weber, Paramount, and the folks at Bad Robot were all very supportive of what we were doing, and understood all the work that went into it. My friend, producer Jeffrey Chernov, is no stranger to makeup and makeup effects. We've now done a number of those films together, so he speaks the language of makeup and was very understanding when we would come to him with, 'Okay, we've got X number of aliens working on this day, so we need X number of artists working through the weekend'. We were never told to back down or ease up in any way; there was always a spirit of comradery between our department, the other departments and production as a whole.

It got to a point one day where we had created 48 different aliens (I know, because I counted them) and my wife Cindy, who worked in the office, said, 'You've got to make 50, because it's the 50th anniversary of *Star Trek*!' It was a brilliant idea! So we ended up making another few aliens. This speaks to what I was just talking about; there was never a sense of, 'Okay, we've got enough!' It was always, 'Let's put another new face or a new character here,' so we would, and by the end we wound up with 56 alien species.

Not only did I know every single character, I knew what prosthetics and accessories went with each of them. I knew which ones needed teeth, quills, fingernails, horns, teeth, eyes, lenses, or whatever it was. I knew every element that went into all of those 56 makeups from the start of prep through additional photography.

When you're looking at the alien makeup of a traditional *Star Trek* series or film, it typically consists of a head and hands, so your focus as an artist/designer is concentrated on facial and head prosthetics and gloves. We wanted to break that mold in this film and, even though you can't redesign the Starfleet uniform too drastically, we could still alter the human shapes beneath with padding and sculptural elements. Apart from the uniforms, we could design characters with much more exposed alien anatomy, so we've got aliens in spaghetti-strap dresses completely covered in prosthetics—and very elaborate prosthetics at that. They still fit into the *Star Trek* world, but an updated version of that.

We also named every one of the characters, and I knew all of them by name. Most of those names came up in the shop where my stepson Bobby and my assistant/coordinator Chris Evitt would start designating them. We always figured they would be renamed when we started filming, but a lot of those names just stuck and therefore appear in the pages of this book. We named them for ourselves, basically just so we could differentiate one from another because there were heads and arms and quills and spines and claws and hair all over the place, so if you didn't know which part went with what other part, it would have been a hodgepodge of random alien elements. Since we were designing and making the aliens, those names were adopted by everybody else. Had we known that these were going to be the final names maybe we would've put a little more thought into them, but it was really just a way to get them all organized in our studio.

Since those names would be on the call sheet every day, I circulated a little cheat-sheet that had all of the character names with their photos. We kept track of all the accessories that went with those names and pictures, so we knew what to bring to set and nothing would get left behind.

What I've done in the upcoming pages is divide up our alien characters based on the locations they're seen in the film. In addition to my own comments, I've included contributions from my own personal 'A-team', including designers Neville Page, Carlos Huante and Allen Williams; sculptors Joey Orosco, Don Lanning, Norman Cabrera, Richie Alonzo, Matt Rose and Mikey Rotella; and my resident 'mad scientist' and problem-solver, Lennie MacDonald…

JAYLAH

DESIGN: NEVILLE PAGE
SCULPT: RICHIE ALONZO

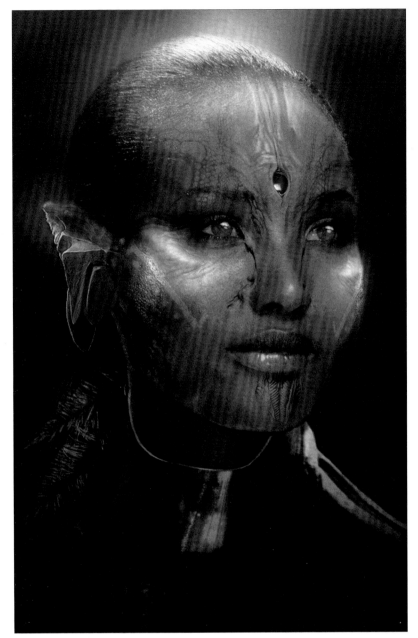

ABOVE: Early concept designs for Jaylah. As the script evolved and the character's role developed, her look changed significantly. The facial ridges on the right-hand image were later used for the Pesca character.

The basic look for Jaylah, including the line work and eyes, definitely came from Neville Page's designs. Carrying the black lines into the hair and having those ridges in the hair was our contribution, but of course with any design, whether it's ours or Neville's or whoever's, it undergoes changes when you translate that design into a practical working makeup. It's almost a second design process, where you've got a guideline but it still becomes its own entity through the process. A design is always intended as a starting point, knowing that concessions and changes will need to be made while still trying to adhere to the spirit of the approved look. The fact that we didn't know who would be playing Jaylah when the design process was started is a perfect example. Clearly, the look will be modified as it is translated to our actress's facial structure.

If you look at the original Jaylah design, it is very striking and beautiful, but it doesn't have eyelashes, for example, and you've got to contend with eyelashes when you're creating a real working makeup because the eyes are the focus of that character, so those are the things you have to consider and adjust to make a design work as a makeup.

When you look at that Jaylah design, it's almost got a lower cleft in the lip, which would have been next to impossible to achieve successfully and still have her

ABOVE: Early Jaylah concepts explored everything from color to skin texture.

perform. Although that element is very interesting in a two-dimensional rendering, it's my job to see the potential pitfalls of something like that, and the mouth is a tricky area for makeup application and prosthetics. When we started translating the concept, we avoided that element because I knew the problems we would be facing over the course of a 78-day shoot. We could push the anatomy when we felt it was practical, but when it's not, it's not. That's part of the *Star Trek* aesthetic: in the real world, there are human beings under these makeups so you try to fool the eye as much as possible, but it's still the performance that is going to sell it.

ABOVE: A set of Jaylah concepts trying out a series of subtle skin patterns.

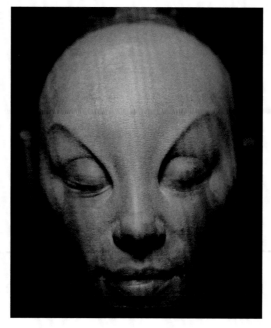

ABOVE: Different angles on the test Jaylah sculpt reveal the placement of the prosthetics.

ABOVE: Richie Alonzo's final Jaylah sculpt incorporated raised areas to ensure each facial marking lined up properly every time.

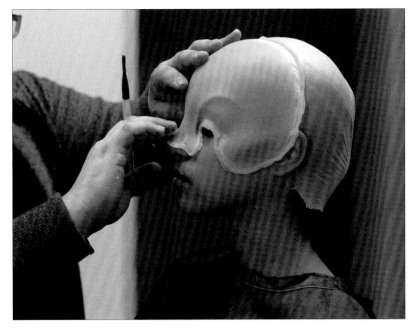

ABOVE: Alonzo applies the Jaylah forehead for test makeup (left); using an airbrush to blend the prosthetics (right).

NEVILLE PAGE: Jaylah was a slam-dunk. That's not because we're great and immediately came up with a design for her, but [the writers] explained who the character was in the script. She's a warrior with a past, who's been stranded and she's very complex. It didn't say she was white with black tribal markings, so that part was wide open. I was the one most involved with her originally, and I hired Joe Pepe to help me out with some designs and he did a fantastic job coming up with a bunch of different iterations.

We presented all our ideas, and round one didn't really resonate. Round two partially resonated, and in round three prior to casting the actress I finally hit one illustration that was it. Once we started going in that direction, I didn't explore a bunch of black and white markings; I did tone and said, 'If you like it, we can explore it further'. That was an example of coming up with an idea they like and you're done; let's do that one. It doesn't often work that way.

ABOVE: Lennie MacDonald and Richie Alonzo test Jaylah makeup on model Demytria Bennett.

"ONE OF THE REASONS THE MAKEUP WAS SO DIFFICULT WAS BECAUSE WE HAD TO MAKE SURE EVERYTHING WAS ALIGNED IN THE RIGHT PLACE."

Richie Alonzo on creating Jaylah

RICHIE ALONZO: Jaylah's look was based off that one design. You knew she was going to be the main character and she had to be elegant and attractive looking, so we said, 'Let's not cover her up so much that you don't recognize who she is, but let the elegance of her face dictate what we need to do!'

We had a forehead appliance that came down on to her cheek areas, which had this patterning, almost like a tattoo pattern, but it was raised from the sculpture. We initially tried it as a paint application and then we were told, 'Let's see if you can do it as a raised tattoo, like a tribal kind of thing,' so we did a sculpture incorporating that idea. It was a tricky makeup because Jaylah had that alabaster/porcelain skin tone, which is always difficult to do because you're covering up her own skin tone,

and you have to make her skin look like skin and then beautify that and then take it even further in terms of the character she's playing, so that was a challenge.

One of the reasons the makeup was so difficult was because we had to make sure everything was aligned in the right place. We had stencils that we followed to make sure everything was in the right place, and the fact that I had done the original sculpture helped a lot because I knew exactly where everything needed to go. I knew where the lines of the tattoo markings had to be, where everything lined up, and what the coloration had to be. We even had a scene at the end of the film where Jaylah had a strapless, sleeveless costume, so I was cringing at the thought of all the body makeup needed to get her ready, not to mention doing her full arms.

 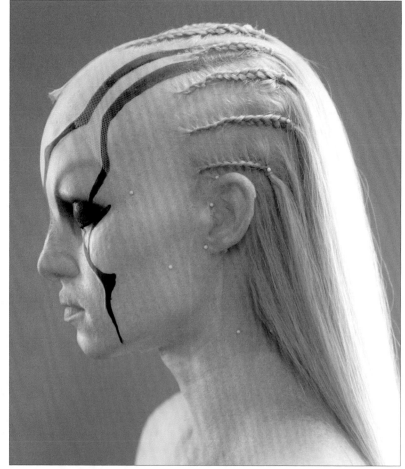

ABOVE: Jaylah's distinctive wig went through a number of color changes before arriving at the final white-blonde look.

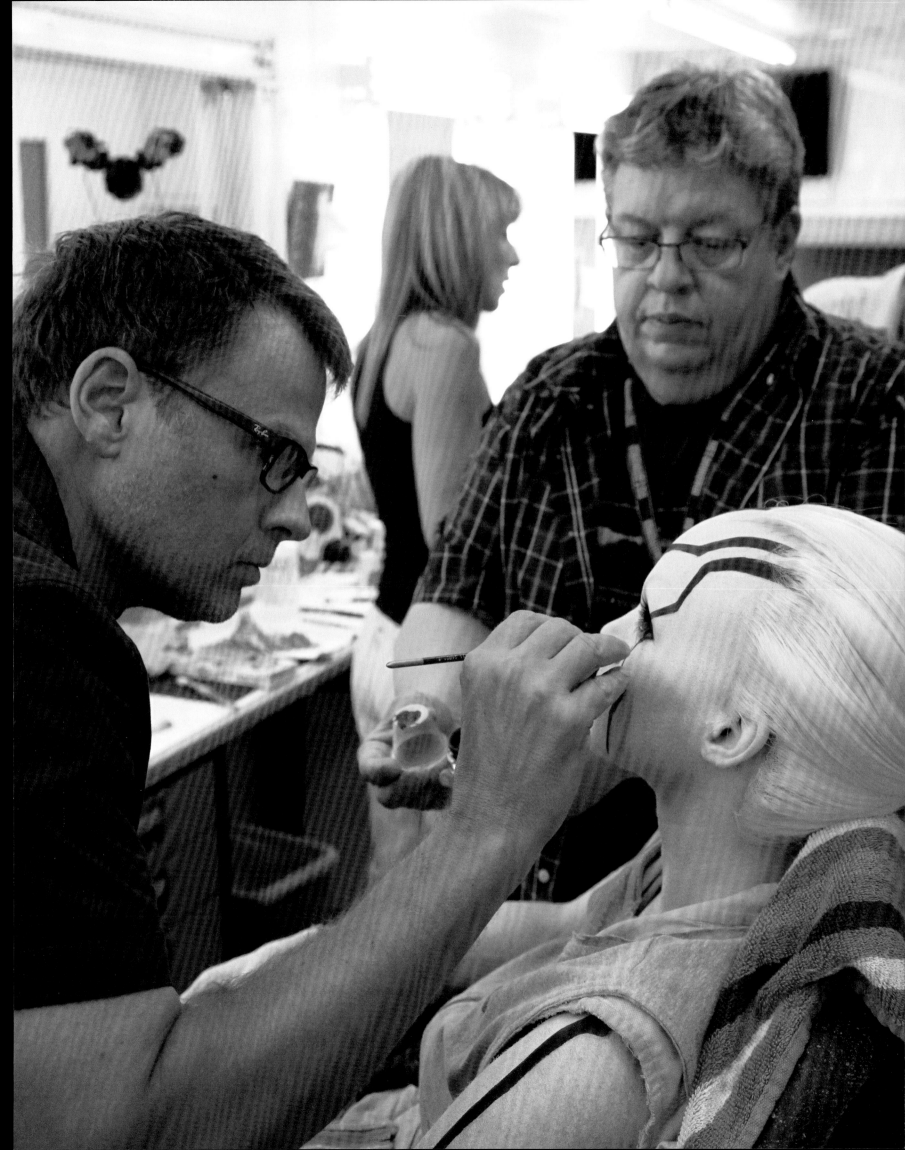

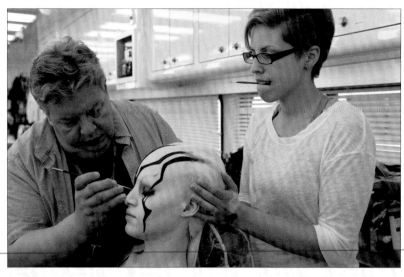

"SOFIA WAS VERY METICULOUS ABOUT LOOKING IN THE MIRROR AND
SAYING, 'THIS LOOKS GOOD!' OR 'THIS MIGHT BE A LITTLE OFF!'"

Richie Alonzo

ABOVE: Early Jaylah makeup/hair concepts saw the character as a brunette.

The prosthetics consisted of one appliance that covers her entire forehead, halfway down the sides of her head and on to the cheekbones. The tattoo lines that go down her cheeks to her jaw line were part of it, so it was very tricky in terms of aligning everything and making sure it all fell into the proper place, but Sofia was very meticulous about looking in the mirror and saying, 'This looks good!' or 'This might be a little off!' It was a very difficult makeup in terms of its simplicity. You think it's simple-looking, but to execute and maintain it through a 14- to 16-hour working day is quite a chore because you have to go back and refresh and fix things, and make it camera-ready again, so that really takes its toll.

Everything had to be flawless and in the right place, and the wig had to be in the proper position. We made templates so that the wig could be aligned properly all the time and an under-foundation was made for the wig so there would be more body, and those ridges of hair that you see on her makeup had to be in exactly the same place each time she worked.

We had pieces that were pre-painted as far as the raised tattoos, and as I did the airbrush painting there was some spatter work and stuff with colors that would overlap onto those black areas, so we would have to go back afterwards and cover any paint spillage and touch up the black areas to make sure they were truly black

BELOW: Numerous makeup tests had to be done for Jaylah to determine color palette and facial tattoo placement.

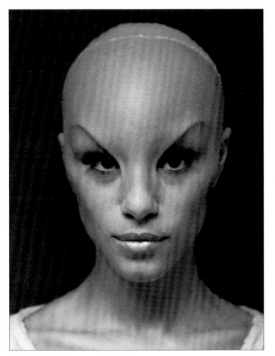

and crisp, so you needed steady hands for that. You can't have the trailer moving or people moving about. There was one day that Joel helped me do her makeup and he said, 'God, now I realize what you were going through!' One mistake on those black lines and you were done, so you had to be really precise about it.

Jaylah originally had a different hair color, and I think she had braids as well. The facial structure and some of the line work was there, but she was more based in flesh tones, so we started off with that and her design evolved from there. Justin kept adding ideas, so she gradually became lighter in skin tone to the point where she went from a brunette with braids to a blonde with blonde hair,

and then her skin started getting lighter in skin tone, almost to a grayish off-white skin tone, and the blonde hair started to look more yellow, which is what happens when you start lightening a skin tone with blonde hair in contrast next to it. The hair starts looking more yellow compared to the skin tone, so Justin said, 'We need to make her hair whiter; we've got to get rid of the yellow!'

In terms of bleaching and trying to make human hair whiter, you can get it to a certain point and it's not going to go any further and it may still have a slight yellow tinge, so our wig maker Khanh Trace was making the wigs, and she said, 'Let me bring in some synthetic hair,' which was a platinum-blonde white. We looked at it and

ABOVE: Hair fabricator Khanh Trace working on Jaylah wigs.

ABOVE: Boutella's makeup had to blend seamlessly into the wig.

ABOVE AND RIGHT: The decision was made to give Jaylah blue blood, rather than red blood.

48

said, 'That looks great!' so she started working on a wig using that hair.

I remember the first day of shooting with Jaylah, she still had the blonde wig and they were going to digitally change the color of her hair. The first scene up was that fight scene with the three aliens in that rock quarry, so I guess they managed to go in and change the color of her hair because we were still in the process of making that wig, so I think we shot one day and the wig was going to be ready the next day, so we switched it out and there was only one day where she had that stage of wig before she had the new synthetic hair. And then Khanh immediately started making another wig, because we had got notice that the first scene coming up was going to be Jaylah. There were going to be two stunt Jaylahs as well, so they were going to need two or three additional wigs for the stunts, so it was the worst thing you wanted at the very beginning of the shoot.

We had fittings with the stuntwomen who were going to be doubling for Sofia, and we fitted the appliances on them and said 'okay, this is going to work'. Then it was a matter of getting the wigs made as quickly as possible, so Khanh managed to pull that off beautifully. Besides Sofia, there were two other Jaylahs they used in that sequence because they wanted to do stuff with holograms of her, and I wasn't sure how visual effects was going to do face replacements for that scene, but they pulled it off.

The very last day of filming was a curveball as well, in the sense that we didn't know she was going to be

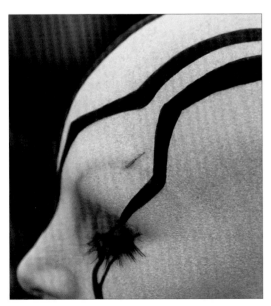

ABOVE AND RIGHT: Even small cuts and scratches revealed Jaylah's blue blood.

THIS PAGE: For Kirk's birthday scene, the character is seen in a casual sleeveless outfit revealing her arm markings as well.

"WE DIDN'T KNOW [JAYLAH] WAS GOING TO BE IN THAT SLEEVELESS OUTFIT UNTIL A DAY OR TWO BEFORE FILMING."

Richie Alonzo

in that sleeveless outfit until a day or two before filming. We knew we would need something for her arms, so we sculpted some appliances that created the same kind of line work as her face, so that's what those appliances became.

The makeup trailer in Dubai wasn't the greatest. Our AC was always breaking down, and the lighting wasn't the best in terms of doing makeup. We were exhausted on that final day because in addition to the Natalia makeup, we were now doing Jaylah and several other characters as well. We had just worked two days back to back, and if we had four hours of sleep in-between, that was a lot. But knowing it was the last day, Joel slept for two hours, took a shower, got dressed and came back to start work on the Natalia makeup, so it was pretty grueling.

Sofia had already finished shooting in Vancouver, but they rewrote the script at the last minute and said, 'Oh, we're going to need Jaylah in Dubai for one more day'. They shot the scene at Starfleet that was also the final scene of the film, and that was literally our last day.

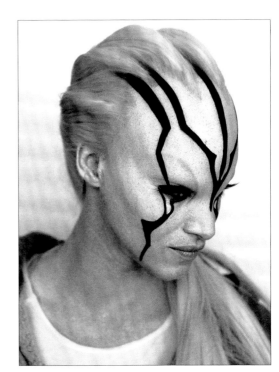

ABOVE: The many faces (and facial tattoos) of Jaylah.

KRALL

STAGE 1
DESIGN: JOEL HARLOW, JOEY OROSCO

SCULPT: JOEY OROSCO

STAGE 2
DESIGN AND SCULPT: JOEY OROSCO

STAGE 3
DESIGN AND SCULPT: JOEL HARLOW

STAGE 4
DESIGN AND SCULPT: JOEY OROSCO

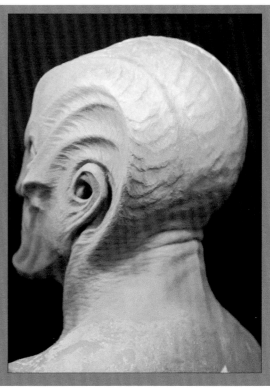

There were sections in the script explaining that Krall had drained the DNA and biological information from other life forms, which dictated the looks for his various stages, starting from the most extreme alien stage and

THIS PAGE: Krall sculptures reveal an incredible amount of detail.

 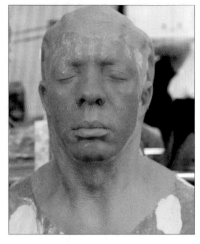 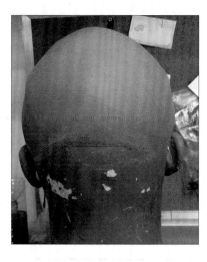 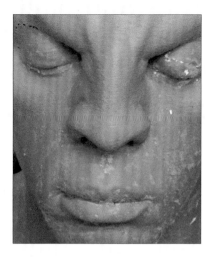

working back down the 'evolutionary' ladder. The first time he drains any human being is when he's got Sulu and Uhura held captive. He takes the essences from two *Enterprise* crewmen, which is visually depicted through a digital effect where he goes through all four stages. We filmed this sequence during our additional photography shoot in Los Angeles.

The second stage unfortunately never made it into the film (beyond glimpses of it in that sequence), and

we went straight to the third stage. You would have seen it much better in the original footage we shot in Vancouver, because he initially drains a crewman in front of the rest of the captured *Enterprise* survivors being marched to the holding pen.

That original confrontation with Sulu and Uhura takes place outside. Krall grabs the 'Cupcake' character (that we did the 'husks' for) and drains him, resulting in his appearance being transformed to what would have been

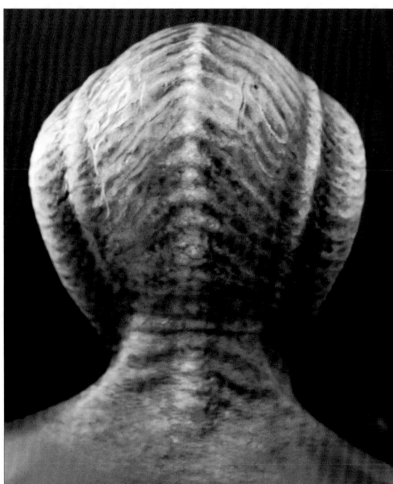

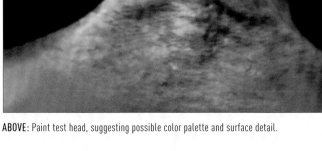

ABOVE: Paint test head, suggesting possible color palette and surface detail.

ABOVE: Michael Fields adds final details to 'stage one' Krall makeup.

"WE THREW IN A LITTLE BIT OF KLINGON, SOME KOMODO DRAGON, MAYBE A LITTLE GILA MONSTER; THOSE SORTS OF SHAPES."

Joel on creating Krall's 'stage one' look

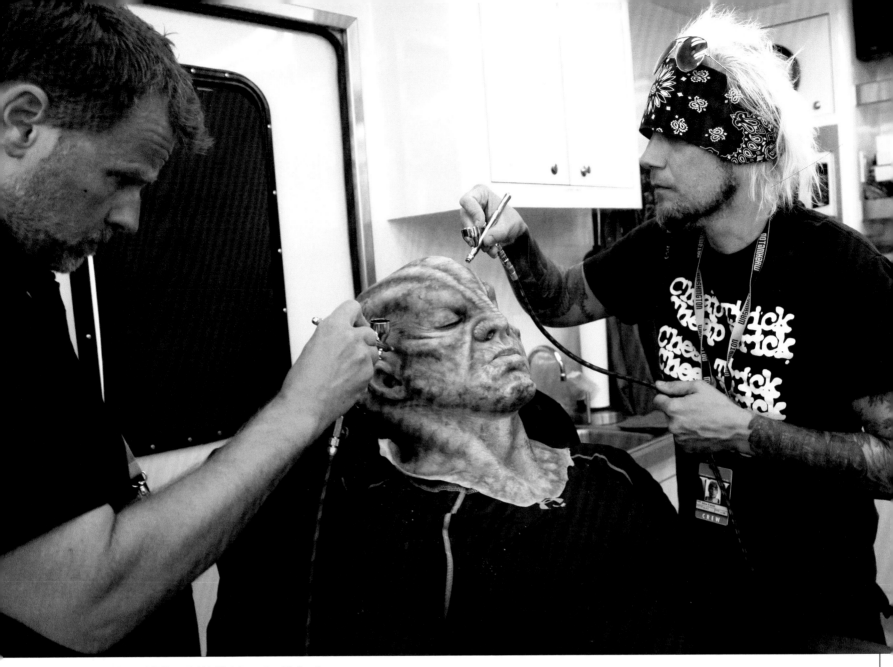

ABOVE: Harlow and Michael Fields apply Idris Elba's 'stage three' Krall makeup.

stage two. As it plays now, we jump to stage three, but of course it isn't noticeable for those unaware that another intermediate stage existed.

Towards the end of the film, when the *Franklin* crashes into and stops Krall's swarm command ship, we see a fully shriveled husk body. We, as the audience, are let in on the fact that Krall has again drained a crewman, who happens to have been a captain. He dons his victim's wardrobe and tries to slip away. It was actually Idris Elba who wanted to do that fourth stage prosthetic makeup because he wanted to appear not completely human. The reason that that subtle final version of Krall exists in the film is because Idris pushed for it. The backstory for Krall is that

he actually started out as a human captain, but over the past 200–300 years he's kept himself alive by draining alien DNA. When he starts draining human DNA, courtesy of the captured *Enterprise* crew, he progressively reverts to a slightly more human form. If he had done it a couple more times maybe he would've ended up as totally human again, but Idris wanted a little bit of that alien still left in him for that end sequence.

Over time, Krall has probably absorbed a multitude of different alien species. Because of that story point, we threw in a little bit of Klingon, some Komodo dragon, maybe a little Gila monster; those sorts of shapes. By comparison, if he had kept draining the DNA of aliens, he probably would have looked even bigger and more distorted as he worked his way through the evolutionary

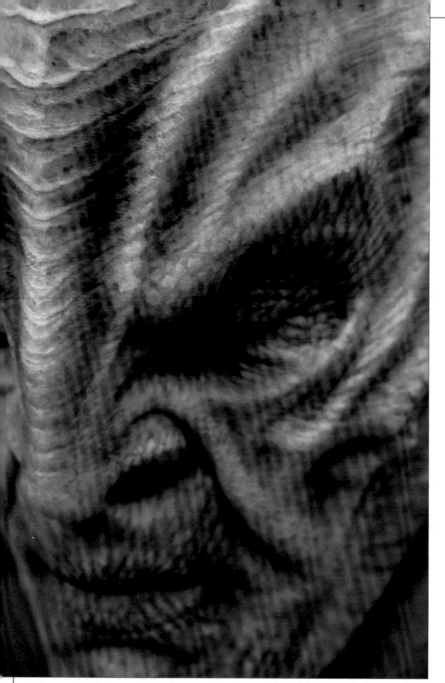

ABOVE: Close-ups reveal the incredible level of paint and sculptural detail that went into Krall's makeup.

ladder, beyond the stage where we see him at the beginning of this film.

There was an initial version of Krall that I had designed, and that Justin had gravitated towards. Everyone sort of fell in line with that particular maquette and started doing different versions of it. For example, Joey Orosco translated one into a full makeup, which was molded and cast, but we never got to apply that version. However, there was just something that didn't feel right about it; the magic was designed out of it, and Justin certainly sensed it as well. He came to the shop and asked, 'Can we address Krall?' This was about two weeks before he was set to start work. All the special elements of this

first version had been worked and re-worked, so it didn't feel right anymore.

At the eleventh hour, we re-addressed Krall and made him into what he is now, which I think is much better than what we had. There was no time to overthink the look at that point, but I think the aesthetic of his look benefitted from that. There's still a raw, wild feeling to the sculpture that works with the nature of the character.

Because we got Idris at the very last minute, the makeup was already finished when he showed up, but fortunately he loved it. He had already worked out the walk and the mannerisms of the character, and our makeup worked with what he was doing and vice versa.

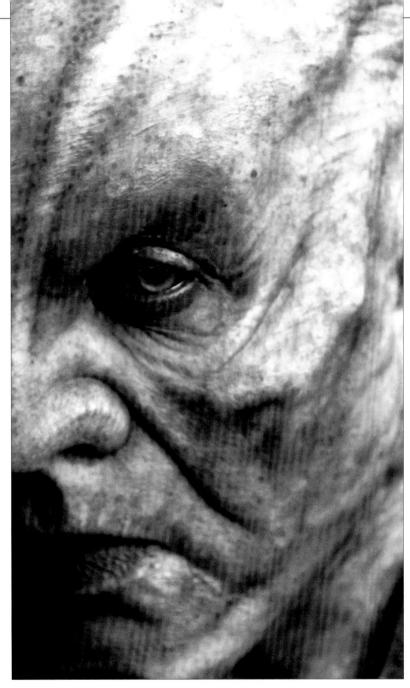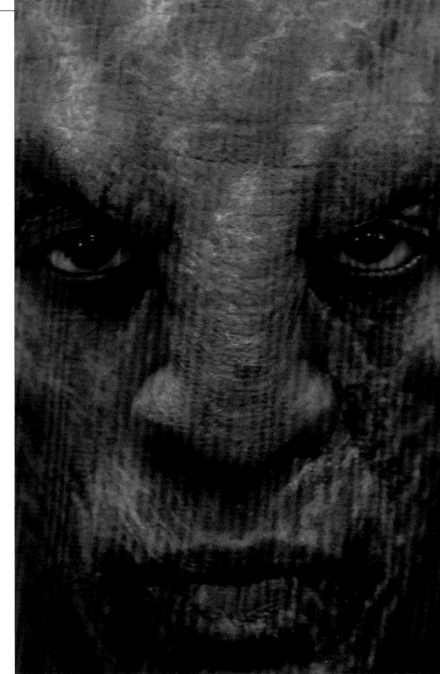

ABOVE: Intermediate stage of Krall makeup (left), and more human stage (right).

I would say the biggest addition to his makeup, which I mentioned earlier, was his request for a stage-four version. Krall was originally going to look human at that point in the film, but with so many aliens walking around Starbase Yorktown we could easily add some alien elements to that look and he could still blend into a crowd. Yet that look isn't so alien that we don't still recognize him as the captain of the *Franklin* we see in the ship's archival footage.

Long before Idris was cast, Joey Orosco had started sculpting the first version of Krall on a generic life cast, but once we got Idris' life cast there was so much re-sculpting that had to be done that Joey basically cut

it up into 14–15 different pieces, which he then had to reassemble like a jigsaw puzzle. This, of course, was the version that was never used, but some of those ribbed design elements were adopted into the Manas character. Had we stuck with the original stage-one design I think there would have been more of a design similarity between those two characters, but in the end the first stage bears more resemblance to Kalara's final look as opposed to Manas. Since these three characters are the only survivors of the *Franklin*, we were conscious about incorporating similar elements into all three, theorizing that they would all be draining the same alien DNA to prolong life, but that it would affect them all differently.

NEVILLE PAGE: Our original conceit was that the character undergoes a major change, but whether or not it was parasitic *a la* the Skeksis of *The Dark Crystal*, sucking the life force out of various species, had not yet been decided. What mattered most was the end result, and once we had that we tried to back up out of it once we had our actor.

We would look at the various transitions, going all the way back to the actor without any makeup, but when you don't have the actor it's a bit difficult to do. Our goal was to figure out what the final, most evolved stage was, so I went about that digitally with a real actor's head. What I've learned is that if you're going to do a makeup design, you can either do pure concept work, where the process can be pencil, digital maquettes, Photoshop rendering; whatever it is, but the problem is when you have a limited amount of time, you've still just created a concept, not a solid idea that can really be used like a makeup test.

Using the knowledge I'd gained from working with J.J. on the Romulans for *Star Trek*, I came up with a virtual makeup using a real actor's head, painting it in CG as though it was a silicone appliance, and rendering it with lighting similar to the set they would actually be on. It meant the director saw a virtual makeup test that would show them what they would get on the first day of production, whereas if I had just done a cool little pencil drawing we would still need to do actual makeup tests

where the director could say, 'I don't know, maybe a bigger nose!', which would be a huge problem financially and time-wise. Frankly, it's not as much fun because I love drawing with a pencil or sculpting with real clay, but it's a much more honest appraisal of what the design should be.

There have been comparisons between Krall and the Klingons in an early design. One of the reasons for that is we had the idea of putting a little Klingon in Krall at some point, because a Klingon might have been one of his victims. With a head makeup, you have to use the actor's eyes, nose, lips and general morphology, so there are only so many landmarks you can play with in terms of shape. And when you have to land within the aesthetic

of an existing franchise, you're mindful of the fact you want to see the actor through the makeup, and when you've got various producers and other people with their own opinions it's even harder to push the envelope as far as doing something we've never seen before. You are then limited to, 'Okay, what can I do with the cheekbones or the ridges on top of the head?'

Believe me, we did some stuff that did not look like Klingons, but *Star Trek* is notorious for certain things such as the forehead, chin and nose. The eyes are off-limits other than contact lenses, and you can't do an awful lot with the head shape because after a while it just becomes a beluga whale of a head. So that's why there was some similarity.

"[JUSTIN LIN] KEPT SAYING 'I WANT TO SEE THESE LINES!' HE KEPT SAYING IT WITH HIS HANDS, THESE LINES, AND HE KEPT RUNNING THEM ACROSS HIS FOREHEAD, SO YOU CAN SEE THEM WHEN YOU LOOK AT KRALL."

Sculptor Joey Orosco on Krall's most 'alien' look

LENNIE MACDONALD: I had done some of the original paint schemes back in LA, when we were playing around with ideas and trying out some light effects inside the head. The original design had a Nautilus-shell look, so when Krall got angry the lights would work inside it. My son, who's really good on the computer, designed the lighting scheme for it. But once we got to Vancouver, the director changed his mind, so we had to redesign, re-sculpt and re-paint everything within an extremely short amount of time. The original sculpture had little panels that went around the head that just called out for that lighting, but once it changed to a different design the idea didn't make as much sense.

That final stage of Krall is very much Joey Orosco. I don't think there were any sketches; it was just Joey sculpting, with Joel and Justin giving feedback. If you give Joey a design, he'll make it even better because he really puts his heart and soul into it. Those are the kind of people I love working with.

Gil Laberto is the guy who made all our molds, and figured how to break things down and make them work as prosthetics, because we were dealing with a lot of weight and stuff like that. I had something to do with it like saying, 'Okay, let's put silk organza into certain things so it doesn't stretch and takes some of the weight', while Gil would deal with issues like with how thick you needed the silicone to be to work properly, and where it could perhaps be replaced with lighter-weight Polyfoam. That's where Gil came in, who's an extremely talented person.

JOEY OROSCO: Joel and I basically created Krall back home in Burbank, and when we got to Canada the director loved what we did, but he had this vision in his head and kept saying, 'I want to see these lines!' He kept saying it with his hands, these lines, and he kept running them across his forehead, so you can see them when you look at Krall. Luckily, the production office was near our shop, so I literally took my sculpture back to the shop and started sculpting again. I said to Joel, 'Let me do something new!' so I really attacked it, thinking about what Justin wanted to see, and within two days I came up this beautiful makeup of Krall. There was no design; that was out of my head with Joel's direction, and I'm really proud of that piece.

There were four different phases for Krall, so there was that first phase, which is a really crazy one. Joel did the middle stage, which you see in the film quite a bit, and I did the final subtle makeup when you see him in the brown makeup when he's fighting.

RIGHT: Krall's most human-looking 'stage', created at Idris Elba's request.

MANAS

DESIGN AND SCULPT:
JOEL HARLOW

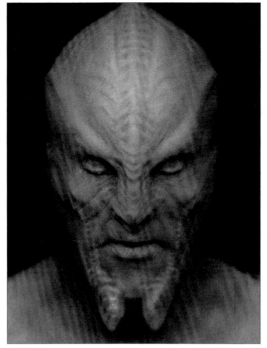

We always knew we would be designing Manas as one of our scripted aliens, along with Krall and Kalara. As it was, the aesthetic of Krall more or less dictated what Kalara and Manas would ultimately look like, even though they were their own individual alien characters. They didn't have to look exactly like the same species, because all three of them were amalgams of many different species of aliens.

It wasn't until Joe Taslim was cast as Manas that I could finally focus on designing him, and I designed and sculpted that character myself. In that process, the only similar feature Manas has to the first incarnation of Krall is the cobra-like hood that radiates out the back of his head and gives him that distinct profile. That was really the only similarity between Manas and Krall; and Kalara too, even though her 'hood' is a bit more ornate and petal-like. I suppose you could argue that a great many of the aliens in this film have similar-shaped craniums, and that was no accident since the concept behind these three is that they would have characteristics of a great many alien species, due to the practice of absorbing alien DNA.

ABOVE: Harlow's early digital concepts explored a wide range of possible looks for Manas.

"SO MUCH OF THAT
MAKEUP AND THAT
CHARACTER IS BASED
ON THE GEOMETRIC
SYMMETRY OF THE HOOD,
CHIN, AND THE VENTS ON
THE SIDE OF THE HEAD
AND CHEEKBONES."

Joel on creating Manas

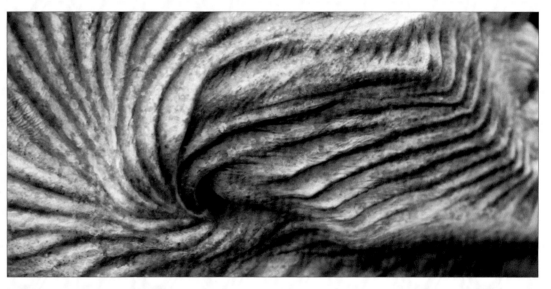

The look of Manas basically came from the many conversations I had with Justin about what he wanted to see before I jumped right into the sculpture, thus there wasn't a lot of two-dimensional design or maquette work for Manas; it was just a matter of jumping right into it. Once I had Joe's face, obviously that dictated a lot of what the makeup could and couldn't be. I didn't pre-sculpt anything for the character until I got his life cast. Justin wanted to see the similarity to Krall, in the sense that they had that same hood/helmet, but Manas also has a bifurcated furrowed chin, which was more prominent in the original Krall. Justin wanted to maintain a version of that chin, which Krall no longer has but Manas does.

In hindsight, I should have broken the makeup down into fewer pieces. The way we broke it down turned out to be nine different pieces. Realistically, there could have been fewer pieces if we had approached the makeup differently. The Manas makeup was a real challenge to apply, while maintaining its symmetry. So much of that makeup and that character is based on the geometric symmetry of the hood, chin, and the vents on the side of the head and the cheekbones, so it was really easy to be off with that symmetry if you weren't completely lined up with the first pieces. Manas was primarily applied by myself and Lennie MacDonald, though sometimes Toby Lindala would apply it with Lennie, but that makeup was a challenge every time we applied it.

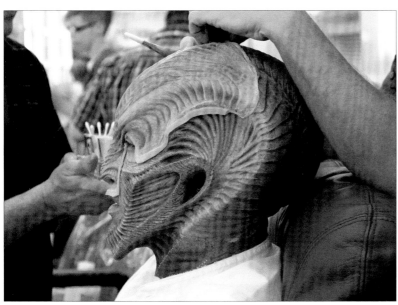

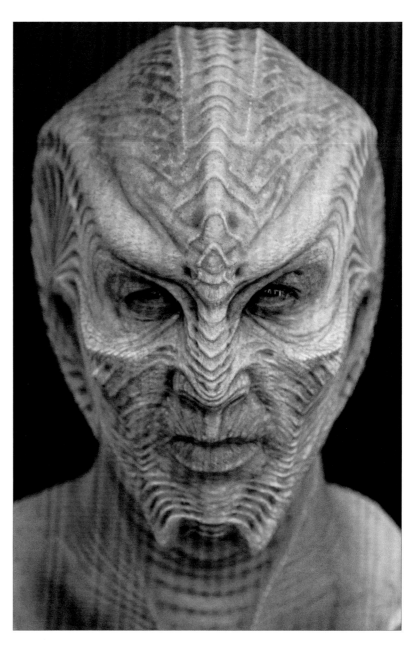

ABOVE: Harlow and Lennie MacDonald applying Manas makeup to actor Joe Taslim.

KALARA

DESIGN AND SCULPT:
JOEY OROSCO

Kalara was a difficult character to conceptualize. She is one of the three surviving crewmembers from the *U.S.S. Franklin*, the other two being Krall and Manas. In the context of the story, these three survivors have managed to stay alive by feeding off of alien DNA. As a result, they have each taken different forms depending on whatever aliens they've been individually draining.

Joey Orosco did the original design for Kalara as a maquette. Once the look was approved by Justin, I had Miles Teves start on the sculpture because Joey was so busy with other characters. We did a couple of makeup tests to work out issues. As we didn't get Lydia (Wilson) until Vancouver to test on, it fell on Joey to re-sculpt the final makeup.

Because Kalara was so smooth looking, there was really no way to break up the face of the makeup, so it had to be one piece (from the forehead to the chin). That made it incredibly difficult to glue down, because you've only got the mouth, the eyes, a little bit of the nostrils, and the sides of the face to glue it all down. Any blend edge would have read if we had separated off the chin or lower lip, so it was very complex to do. It was mostly myself and Toby Lindala applying that makeup together, every day. We broke it down into three pieces, so there was a cowl, a face, and a neck wattle area that blends into the cowl at the neck.

When Joey started working on Kalara, the first version of Krall was already moving along, so the silhouettes are quite similar. You could say she's almost a more elegant version of Krall, and if you look at her now with the fins on her head she bears more resemblance to the screen-used first stage of Krall, which is interesting because she actually came before him.

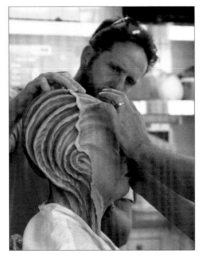
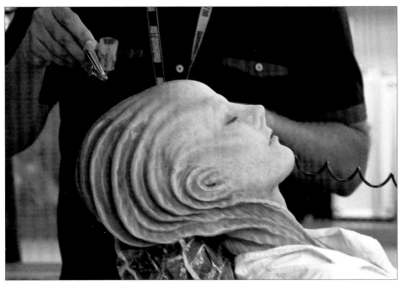

ABOVE: Toby Lindala and Harlow turn Lydia Wilson into Kalara.

ENSIGN SYL

DESIGN: NORMAN CABRERA

SCULPT: NORMAN CABRERA & JOHN WRIGHTSON

ABOVE: Norman Cabrera's Syl concepts show a heavy Giger influence.

I had a meeting with Justin based on some script revisions, which required an alien character whose anatomy was designed to hide the Abronath in, which is that piece of planet-destroying technology Krall is after. I had Norman Cabrera do a maquette of an alien with its head in both an opened and closed position. We decided to give a nod to H.R. Giger in the concept by giving the back of the head a 'facehugger' look. Justin signed off on it right away, so that's what we went with, and Norman sculpted the makeup on Melissa Roxburgh's life cast.

A lot of the credit goes to Lennie MacDonald, who devised the head in such a way that it could open and close with armature wire and brass tubing. The 'fingers' wouldn't move on camera, but you could position them in an open or closed position. He also designed the inside of the back of the head with a magnet that allowed the Abronath to pop in and out.

ABOVE: Lennie MacDonald double-checks Syl's opened head elements.

RIGHT: Harlowe MacFarlane and Richie Alonzo apply Melissa Roxburgh's Syl makeup.

LENNIE MACDONALD: The Ensign Syl character was loosely based on the H.R. Giger character we built for the movie *Species*, and is a sort of homage to the facehugger, which was her 'hair' that opens up, revealing this object they've hidden there, which they can then remove. We made it so the fingers of the hair were closed the whole time, but Joel had me make a poseable version the actress could wear, and they wanted it to look like it was closed too, so I had to do several different things with it.

I made a wire armature that could be reset, and put a magnet inside the thing in her head. The prop was magnetized too, so it was like a magic trick where it just came out easily. We filmed it open and closed, and they digitally enhanced it opening, but we gave them as much information as possible. At the end, I had to literally stitch her head into a closed position to make it as tight as it needed to look. Norman had worked on *Species* at Steve Johnson's shop, sculpting the lead character, so this was a little shout-out to Sil and to Giger.

ABOVE: The Syl 'fingers' were sculpted in an open and closed position.

NORMAN CABRERA: Joel came to me and said, 'We're doing this alien character that basically has to hide an object in its head'. I thought about it and said, 'You know, it would be cool if it had wrapped-up fingers on the back of the head!', so that's what I suggested and Joel thought it sounded cool. I also referenced Giger's work, and the artist Beksiński, who did a lot of stuff with fingers and hands and multiple limbs.

I did a maquette based on the idea of these fingers holding in this intergalactic egg, so probably more subconsciously than not it ended up looking like a facehugger, but that really wasn't a conscious thing. And if you looked at the maquette, there's a wild-looking woman from the film *Metropolis* who had a headdress or hair that almost looked like futuristic cornrows, so I infused a bit of that into the design of the character too. None of this was premeditated; as artists, we glean inspiration from all these different references and the end product is the culmination of all those things. Because I had to leave the project at the end just before it finished, John Wrightson sculpted the area inside the fingers, but it was still designed by me. I did a closed version and an open version so you could see what it looked like.

BELOW: Syl arm detail.

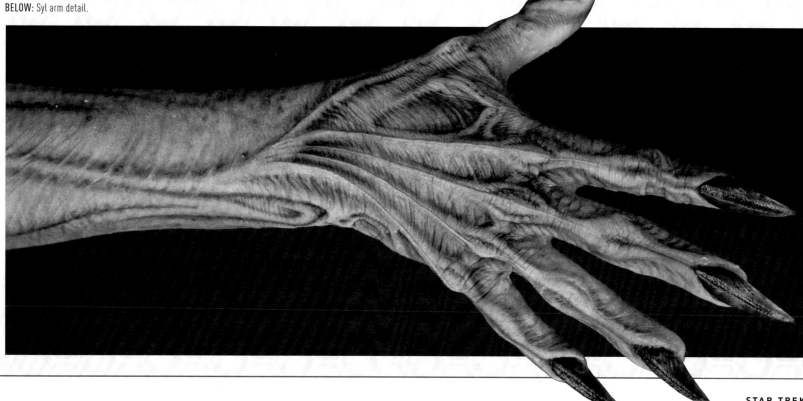

KEENSER

DESIGN & SCULPT:
DON LANNING

Don Lanning designed and sculpted this character for the first film, and those molds were used on the second film as well. By the time we got to those molds for this film, however, they were virtually unusable. The molds were made out of Bondo-resin and because of that, the seams were getting worse as the years passed, so it quickly became apparent that the prosthetics for Keenser would need to be redone. Don is a replicating machine. He had expressed a desire to clean up the sculpture and refine the detail, so this afforded him the

opportunity to do that. He also sculpted new hands for Deep Roy to complete the makeup, so it's been completely redone based on what Don felt it needed back on the first film.

Looking back, we probably would have redone the Keenser molds anyway, just because we wanted everything to be new. To have 50-plus different aliens and have one of them a holdover from another film just didn't feel right, so we wanted to make everything new from sculpture onward.

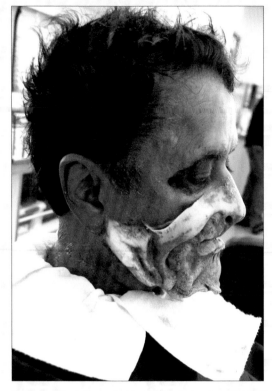

ABOVE: Deep Roy in Keenser facial prosthetics; two angles of finished head piece.

DON LANNING: I designed the character for the original 2009 movie and Joel knew that. It was one of those characters I sent over to J.J. and got approved, so I was very happy to be involved with the re-sculpt of it because even though I had designed the maquette, I didn't sculpt the original makeup. Barney Burman had done that as the show was changing hands from him to Joel, so I think that was a nod to me because Joel was there at the time and had seen me do it.

RIGHT: Deep Roy gives the new Keenser makeup his seal of approval.

BELOW: Don Lanning tweaks his finished Keenser sculpture.

TY VANA

DESIGN: ALLEN WILLIAMS

SCULPT: MILES TEVES, JOEL HARLOW & JOEY OROSCO

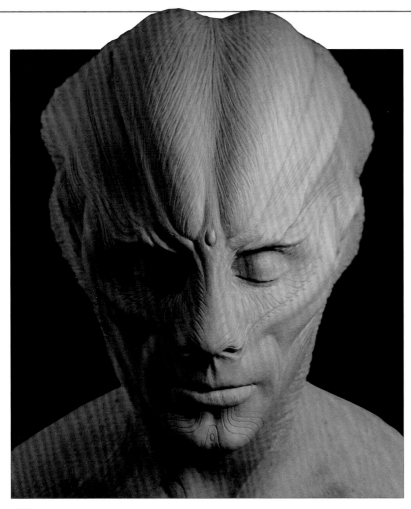

ABOVE: Ty Vana sculpture in progress.

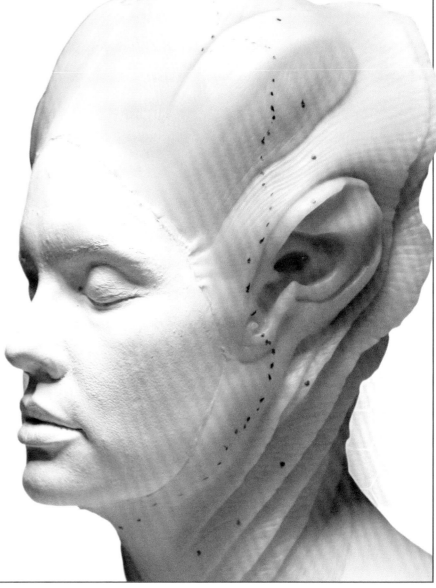

We see this character, played by Anita Brown, on the deck of the *Enterprise*. Before production found Anita, we had already molded the back of her head, which was sculpted on a life cast of Chris Evitt (one of our shop runner/technicians). However, we hadn't molded the face yet. When we got Anita in Vancouver, we took her life cast and applied the cowl piece on the back and re-molded the face. I jumped in to do some of the sculpting, changing the structure of the face to make it more feminine. This character also had fins and accessory pieces, which extended the back of the head even further. We ran these fins out of a Water Clear silicone so that you could see through them.

There are two versions of this character: a pink-and-purple version, and a green-and-yellow version that played in Dubai on a background artist. In both cases I think the paint job helps sell the character and really helps the sculpture along.

RIGHT: The finished cowl prosthetics on lifecast, ready for new face snap.

ALLEN WILLIAMS: I see Ty Vana as the female version of another character I designed, which is Satine, the Venus flytrap-headed guy. The patterns on her face are basically the same, but they made Ty Vana a female while Satine was switched over to a masculine character. You can think of them as a male and female version, but maybe the males have the spines on their heads!

RIGHT: Ty Vana was partially designed as a female counterpart of Satine (above).

ABOVE: Werner Pretorius (top) and Lennie MacDonald (bottom) work on final paint scheme for two different versions of Ty Vana (right).

ORION GIRL

DESIGN: JOEL HARLOW

ABOVE: Director Justin Lin, a big fan of the original TV series, was keen to have an Orion girl in his film.

'm not exactly sure if it was Justin or Lindsey Weber at Bad Robot who wanted an Orion girl in the film somewhere, but it was certainly an easy enough thing to achieve. There was no molding or sculpting involved; it's simply a paint job, a beauty makeup and a wig, so it certainly didn't take the hours of lab time that some of the other characters took.

The big difference with our Orion girl and the ones in previous *Star Trek* TV shows and films was the shade of green we used for her. The other Orion girls had always bothered me, because they looked like makeup. They didn't have the depth of skin breakup and realism that we were shooting for.

We wanted her to look real, but we were also dealing with the aesthetic of the film as a whole. This is three years into the crew's five-year mission, whereas in the last two films the *Enterprise* looked very new and pristine. The idea and the art direction of this film was that the *Enterprise* would now feel a little worn in and a little duller as far as the sheen on everything was concerned, so that was taken into account when we did the Orion girl. We didn't want her to pop or be too vibrant. We wanted it to feel like a real skin color. It wouldn't be neon green; it would have layers just like human skin, no matter what color it was.

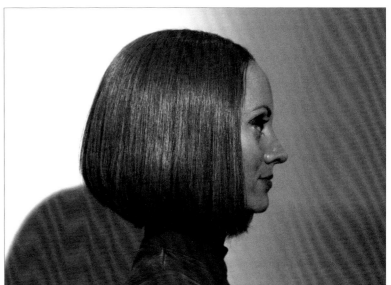

ABOVE: Harlow wanted this film's Orion girl to have a more subdued, 'realistic' color palette than previous versions.

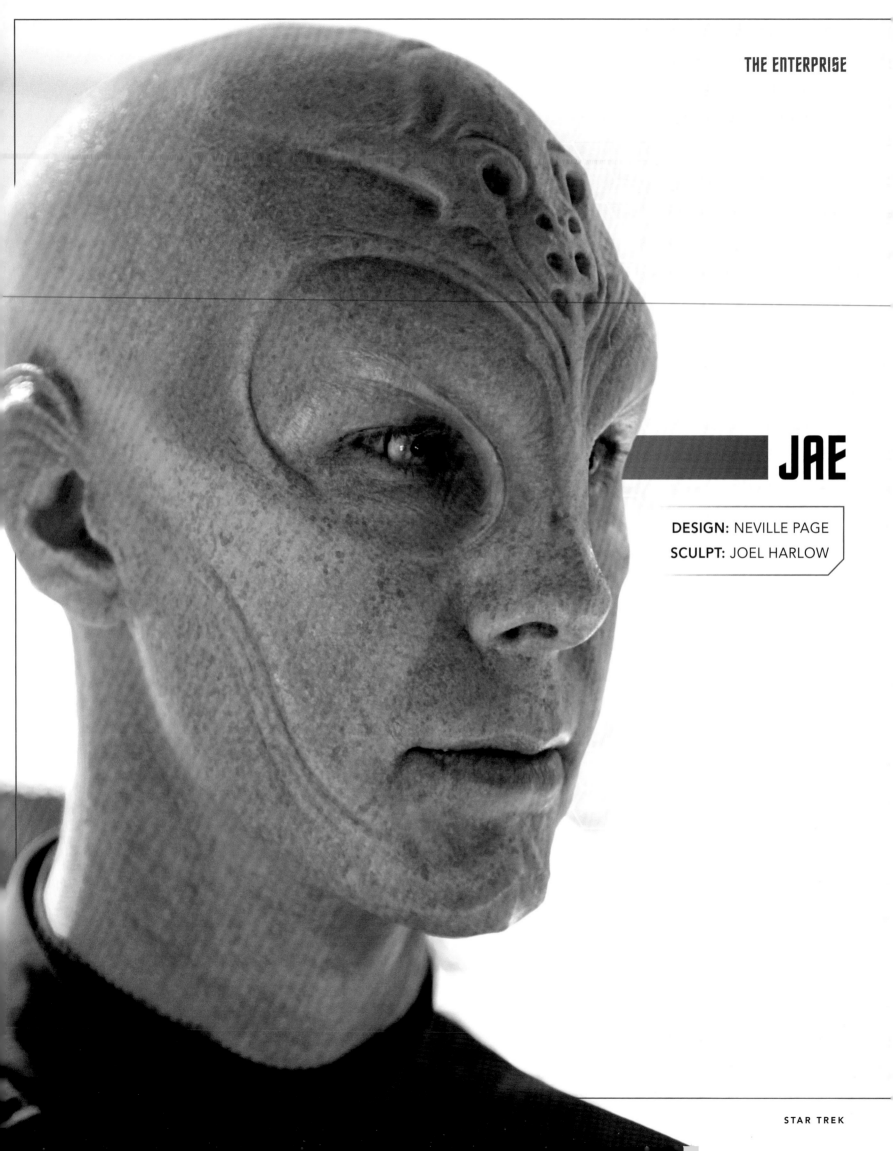

JAE

DESIGN: NEVILLE PAGE
SCULPT: JOEL HARLOW

ABOVE: Original Jae sculpt (left) and finished makeup with head disc (right).

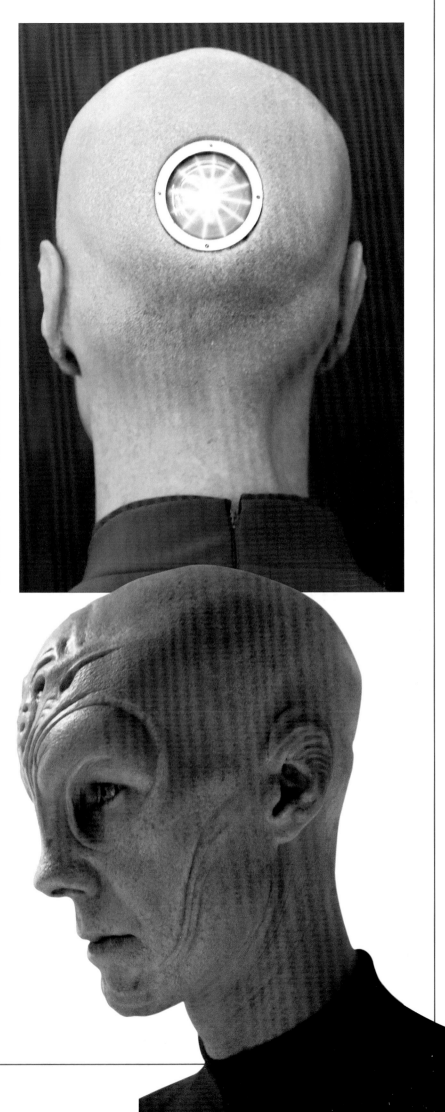

Jae started off as a bartender character in the early scripts, but ultimately he ended up on the bridge of the *Enterprise*; his station is to Kirk's left when he's sitting in the captain's chair. He's a different version of another character from the previous film, who had a little disk on the back of his head. He's bald and doesn't have any eyebrows, and he's got piercing blue eyes; he almost looks like a robotic character. He is on the bridge of the *Enterprise* in *Into Darkness*, so this was a new version of that character.

We really didn't want to reuse anything so I handled re-sculpting the prosthetics for this character. There was one point when we were going to reuse one of the aliens from the bar sequence in *Into Darkness*, but it wasn't necessary because we already had so many characters.

STATIC

DESIGN: JOEL HARLOW

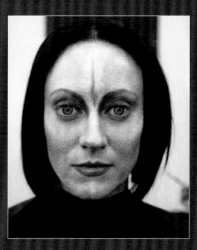

We didn't do a sculpture for this character; it's another painted alien character. I think in lieu of the Jae alien on the bridge, we were going to put this character in there instead. It was almost an android kind of character, but the actress that played her ultimately became the green Orion girl. That was the first pass at that character. We did a lot of tests in the beginning of different things, and this was one that ultimately did not make it into the film.

THIS PAGE: Paint scheme designs for Static, one of the film's 'painted' (as opposed to prosthetic-based) aliens.

SPOCK SCULPTURE

This amazing bust of Leonard Nimoy as Spock isn't from the film; it was a memorial and a thank you to a small group of production people. It was done off a life cast of Leonard that we took on the first re-booted film. I had Joey sculpt the eyes open, add highlights, wardrobe and hands for the piece. It's a beautiful tribute.

Even if you don't know *Star Trek*, you still know Spock. He's iconic. Mindy Hall and I applied his makeup together on the first film. I was responsible for applying the ears, while she did the eyebrows. We would flip-flop on the sides of the face. Leonard knew those ears better than anyone—he knew the correct angles, both in terms of the curvature in towards his head and towards the front of the head. He even knew how the tips should curve; he knew more about those ears than anybody on the planet.

I must have sculpted six different versions of those ears until I finally got them right to his eye, and of course I sculpted in all the age that those ears would have accumulated since the last film. The first time we put him in full makeup, hair and wardrobe was pretty amazing because suddenly here was Spock. At the end of every day, we would take off the ears and he would save them so he could auction them off for charity. He was, simply put, a great man and a pleasure to work with.

We engineered those ears to be literally seamless. Every ear he wore before had a seam, because they were made of foam latex. These were seamless silicone ears, and Leonard paid me probably the biggest compliment I've ever received in my career when he told me they were the best ears he had ever worn. That meant a lot, because I was trying to do right by him and the fans.

RICHIE ALONZO: I was on the first film when Leonard came in to get made up as Spock. It was so exciting to meet him, and so nice to hear him speak. Joel would ask for feedback about what Leonard liked and didn't like, trying to get his makeup to the point where he was totally happy with it, and that's the makeup you see in the first film. As a kid, watching him on TV and then getting to actually meet him, that's something indelibly marked on your memory.

JOEY OROSCO: We were just getting started in Burbank when Joel said, 'Dude, when we're finishing up the show, I want you to sculpt a Leonard Nimoy piece!' At that point, Joel and I had never even met before. The sculpture started out as a really horrible life cast that we had, but I was able to use it and went on from there to create the final sculpture. Joel was very involved with the positioning of it and what he wanted to see, so I just went for it.

I thought about his family and the fans, and what they would want to see. The whole thing with him touching his heart came from Joel, who wanted me to make sure Spock's hand was touching his heart, and I really loved that idea. I literally sculpted that piece in maybe four days, and it was the very last thing I did on the show. I put myself in a little secret area where nobody could see what I was doing, but one of the producers walked in and said, 'Oh, what's that?' so Joel had to tell him it was a gift. I was really lucky to be able to do that sculpture.

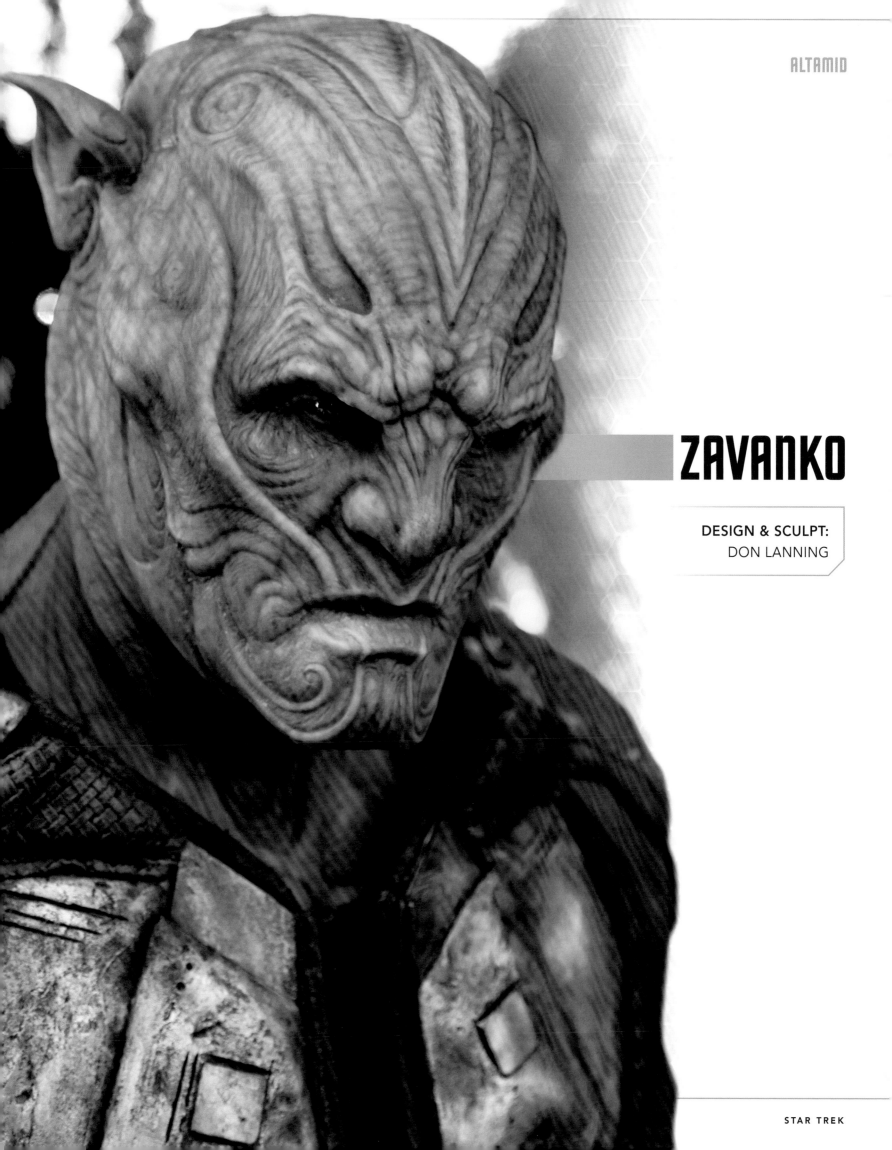

ZAVANKO

DESIGN & SCULPT:
DON LANNING

I actually saw the name 'Zavanko' in a magazine and thought, 'That's the name!' Before that, we were just calling him 'Scavenger', or referring to him as 'Kim Kold', who is the actor who played him. Don Lanning did a little maquette with some intricate scrollwork on its face. Norman Cabrera took that image and translated it into the J-9 and Jin makeups. They became male and female versions of the same character and were painted completely differently from this character, so they became their own race while Zavanko became his own race. Initially, however, they all started from the same original concept.

What really made the character so outstanding for me was the paint job by Lance Webb, which looked almost like dripping rust, alluding to the fact that it was almost an Art Deco piece when it was taken with the line work. Don also sculpted a pair of arms for the character, one of which had a three-dimensional branding tattoo on it, but they were all done with this alien scrollwork element in them.

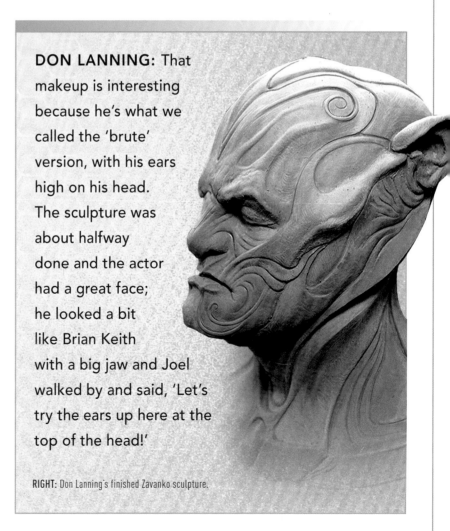

DON LANNING: That makeup is interesting because he's what we called the 'brute' version, with his ears high on his head. The sculpture was about halfway done and the actor had a great face; he looked a bit like Brian Keith with a big jaw and Joel walked by and said, 'Let's try the ears up here at the top of the head!'

RIGHT: Don Lanning's finished Zavanko sculpture.

QUILLS

DESIGN & SCULPT:
DON LANNING

ABOVE: From left to right: Don Lanning's Quills sculpture, an early makeup test, finished prosthetics before quills are added.

This was another character designed for the first script. There was originally going to be an ice planet, so we were going to create more of a walrus-type alien. At that point, Don Lanning was still sculpting out of his own studio in Van Nuys; I went over to his space and blocked out half of the face on a miniature sculpting bust he had created. I spread the eyes out and tweaked the shapes a bit, and he matched it on the other side, so I guess we designed it together. Don translated it to the full-size version and sculpted the hands, which were mechanized by Tim Ralston, being designed to slave off of the actor's fingers via rings.

I still wanted something else for the character, though, so I thought, 'Okay, what else can we put on him to take it to the next level? Do we use hair, feathers, spines, horns, quills? Oh yeah, quills would be nice. The head has these deep pores, so let's go that route with it and make it look more like a porcupine than a walrus!'

Lennie MacDonald then spent a great deal of time cutting the vinyl cords that come out the bottom of Weed Whackers to the right length, sanding them down into points and using them as quills, which was very clever as they were very flexible and so wouldn't cause any damage if they accidentally came into contact with any of the other actors. This was a different environment now; instead of an ice planet, it's now a forest, where this character and his fellow scavengers first meet Jaylah and a fight ensues.

ABOVE: Harlow demonstrates Quills' animatronic hand extensions.

LENNIE MACDONALD: The final character looked more like a porcupine than a walrus, so I did some painting on that character and added the quills. We basically took the nylon you use for a weed eater, cut them at a certain angle and sanded them all down so they had a tapered end. They also had a degree of flexibility to them and I cut them in at least five different sizes that were punched into the foam rubber, so Quills was a combination of silicone and foam rubber.

The part of his face that went over his lips and nose was silicone. The reason we did that was that when we were sculpting, we didn't know who the actor was going to be. We picked Ryan Reynolds because we had his life cast from *Green Lantern*, but when we got the actual actor, his head was much bigger so it wasn't going to work, but if we combined foam rubber and silicone we might be able to make it work. Silicone is usually bigger than you need it to be, while foam rubber is usually smaller. The foam kept shrinking, so we were literally hollowing it out from the inside to make it fit, and stretching the silicone as far as possible to just make it to the edge.

DON LANNING: We basically switched the muzzle sculpture when it was no longer a walrus, so Joel sculpted a new muzzle from the upper lip to the eyes. I did a cleaner variation, and he did one with heavier wrinkles. We were also able to get a very different effect by changing the paint jobs and moving certain facial appliances, like the upper lip.

THIS PAGE: Lennie MacDonald and Carolyn Williams (below) apply the Quills makeup.

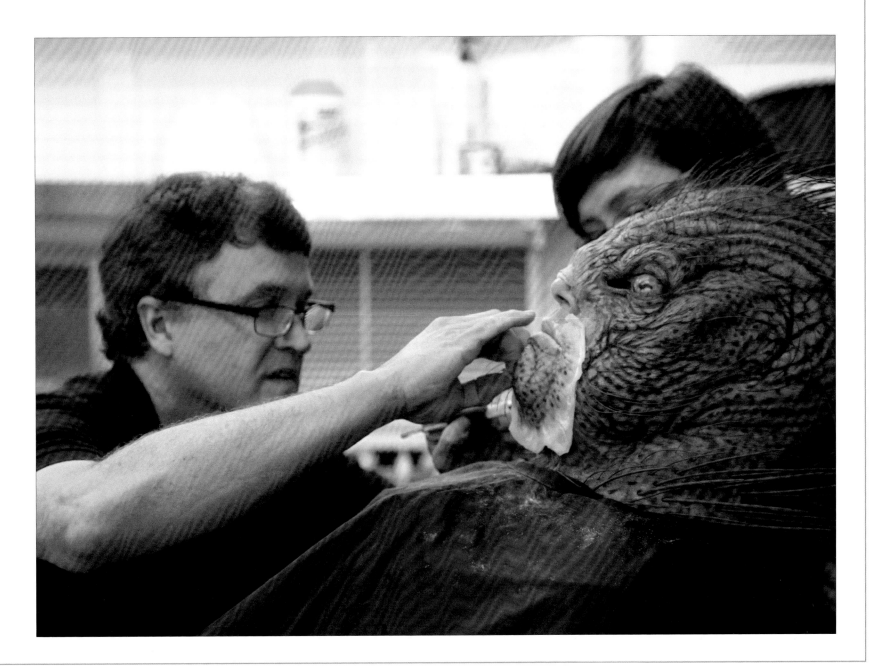

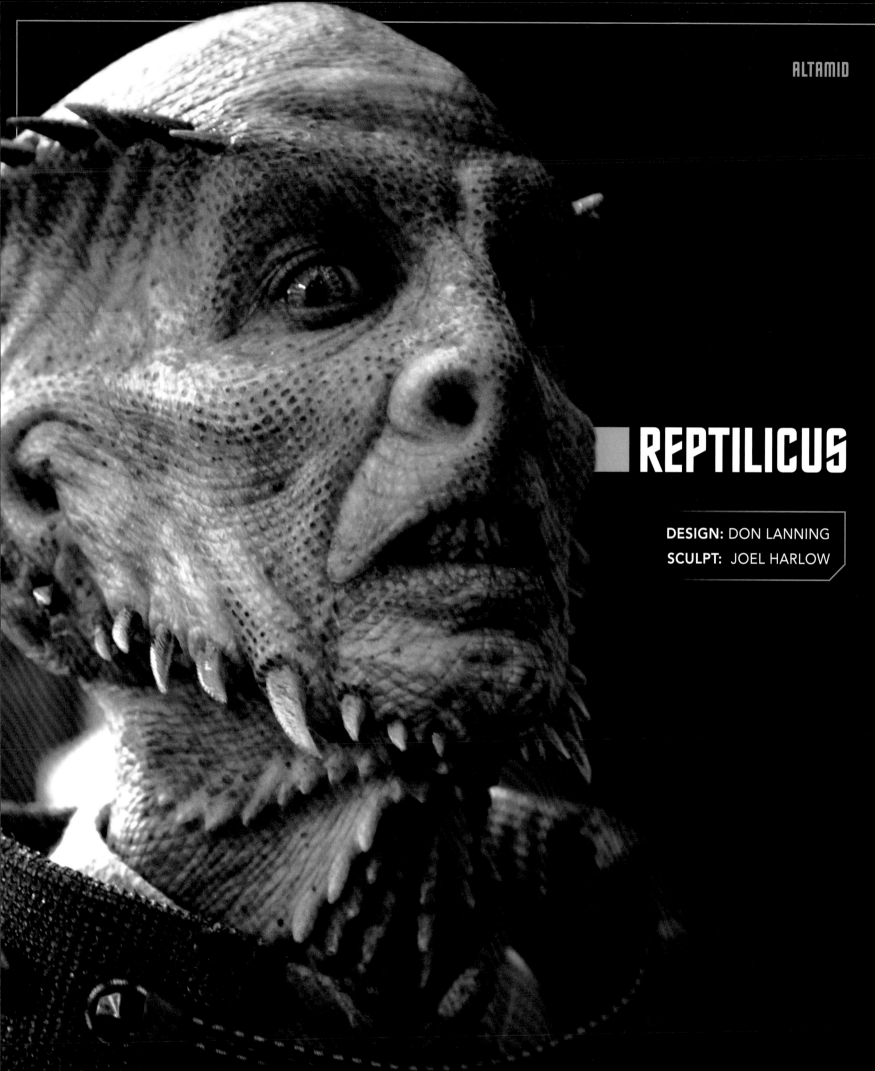

REPTILICUS

DESIGN: DON LANNING
SCULPT: JOEL HARLOW

ABOVE: Harlow applies Reptilicus makeup.

ABOVE: Michael Fields touches up stunt makeup on location.

That's a design that Don Lanning and I did together. Don finished a little maquette of it, but I sculpted the actual makeup and applied it with Felix Fox. The character, who is credited as Fi'Ja, was played by Danny Pudi. Danny was absolutely fantastic, but very different from the generic life cast I had initially sculpted over. Danny is quite thin, while I believe the life cast I sculpted on was Ryan Reynolds, so it was completely different from Danny's neck width and head shape. I actually think

it worked much better on Danny because he's leaner and, when in the prosthetics, feels more lizard-like.

I initially had a tongue made for the character so that he would be able to flick it in and out, but I quickly realised that to have him wear it all day, especially if there was going to be any dialogue involved, just wasn't going to be practical. That's one of my favorite characters. Since I sculpted that one myself, I really sank my teeth into it.

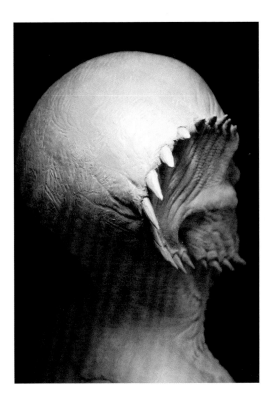

ABOVE: Three different angles of Harlow's finished Reptilicus sculpture.

WADJET

DESIGN: NEVILLE PAGE
SCULPT: JOEY OROSCO

ABOVE: Finished Wadjet makeup, along with Joey Orosco's original sculpture of the character.

elieve it or not, 'Wadjet' is the name of an Egyptian snake god. That character was the first thing Joey Orosco sculpted when we were just setting up the shop in Burbank. It was still just bare bones, but I had a life cast of Scotty Ian, the guitar player from Anthrax, as I had previously done a couple of makeups on him. I just brought out all my generic head casts and we all started sculpting on them since most of our aliens wouldn't be cast until months later in Vancouver. Joey grabbed Scott's life cast and started sculpting the Wadjet character on it, translating what was a pretty ornate Z-Brush design by Neville Page into a fantastic sculpture.

The makeup for that character was not easy to apply, and of course it was generic, so once we got up to Vancouver it was difficult to find somebody to fit it on. We ultimately found a gentleman named Dan Payne, who wore it beautifully and really sold the makeup with his performance. The character actually gets some good screen time—he's in the holding pen with Sulu, Uhura and the rest of the captured crew. Holland Miller did the beautiful pre-painting, I again did the test application, and on the shoot day it was primarily Kevin Haney, who we brought up to Vancouver for some of our big quarry sequences, who did the application.

ABOVE: Joey Orosco sculpts Wadjet on a generic lifecast of Anthrax guitarist Scott Ian.

ABOVE: Harlow and Holland Miller test Wadjet makeup on actor Dan Payne.

JIN AND J-9

DESIGN & SCULPT:
NORMAN CABRERA

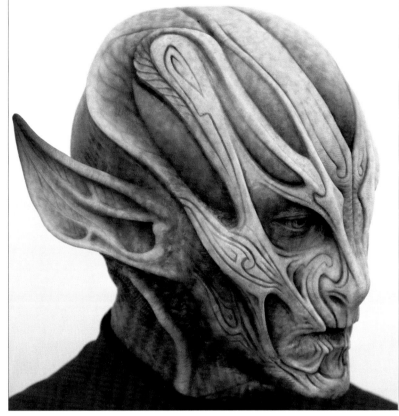

ABOVE: J-9, the female scavenger (above) and Jin, the male scavenger (right).

These two aliens started out as Zavanko, the scavenger character that Don Lanning was sculpting. He did a maquette with some interesting scrollwork on the face, and Norman Cabrera took that element and translated it into the Jin and J-9 makeups (Jin being male and J-9 female). It's strange to compare them to Zavanko now, especially as they were pre-painted completely differently. I think that stage is when they became their own race, but they all began as the same concept.

J-9 is the female alien, being short for Jeanine, the actress who played her. She gets captured by Krall and the *Enterprise* crew liberates her. Jin is the male, and there are actually two of them. The one in the holding cell is played by Anthony Shim, painted with an earthy color palette. The other Jin was played by Luca Hays, costume designer Sanja Hays' son. He was painted by Lennie MacDonald in iridescent purples and blues.

Half the fun of this film was creating characters you hadn't seen before. Since the timeline was reset after the first film, we weren't limited to characters that fans have come to expect from *Star Trek* films, so these characters are two excellent examples of new alien life forms.

ABOVE: Early concepts show the visual link between Jin, J-9 and Zavanko.

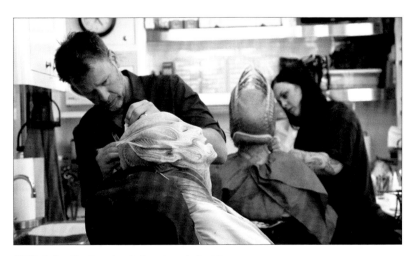

ABOVE: Joel applies the makeup to the actress playing J-9.

ABOVE: Jin and J-9 were sculpted by Norman Cabrera, who brought similar design elements to both characters.

NORMAN CABRERA: When Joel originally talked to me about fleshing out those characters, they were just called 'the Scavengers,' and Don had done an initial maquette for them with these large animal ears. With every character you do, you've got to attach a backstory to make it believable, so the thinking here was, if they were scavenger-type aliens relying on their senses to find things, they would have these large animal ears. Joel said, 'Take this idea of these scavengers with large animal ears and run with it!' so I started with the female and then the male, and they developed sculpturally as they went along. I would start moving the clay around, and Joel would come up behind me and start giggling like a kid in a toy store, so I would get even more excited, and that would perpetuate the process of designing the character.

RIGHT: Steve Buscaino touches up Anthony Shim's Jin makeup.

RIGHT: Finished J-9 makeup, showcasing Harlow's iridescent paintwork.

MERELL AND MARTI

DESIGN: NEVILLE PAGE
SCULPT: JOEL HARLOW

These two characters were included in the pick-up shoot. We didn't actually create any new aliens for those additional scenes, but the Merell character, for example, was never in the film until the additional photography. Ironically, it was one of the first aliens I sculpted and one of the first we tested (on my stepdaughter Ashley Edner). There was a chance it was going to be used for the Jaylah character, but with the script still in flux that character got shelved, so I brought her back when we did the re-shoots. I believe you see the character in one of the scenes after the *Enterprise* is destroyed and some of the escape pods are captured, and the same with Marti.

SATINE

DESIGN: ALLEN WILLIAMS
SCULPT: MATT ROSE

ABOVE: Michael Fields (above) and Carolyn Williams (right) work on different versions of the Satine head.

When I got this design from Allen Williams, I initially didn't see its full potential. There was something that just didn't feel dimensional enough about it to me, but it was a design that Justin gravitated towards. Once Matt Rose began sculpting it and putting his magic into it, it began to feel more like a character and I could see the brilliance of what Allen had done. Don't get me wrong, Allen is an amazing illustrator; he's easily one of the best I've ever seen, but I think he was playing around with Z-Brush and this was one of those early designs. It became one of my favorite characters, it's got something so alien about it when you see the finished version; certainly the paint job helps tremendously.

I had the idea of putting the quills in the top of the head and the chin, and turning it into more of a Venus flytrap sort of character, something that was more plant than animal. We didn't have any plant characters in this movie yet, so it felt natural, especially because the way it was painted made it feel like more of a plant-type alien. Rob Hinderstein created the eyes for it, which were fantastic, and Lennie MacDonald worked out the mask underneath to hold the eyes in place via magnets, so we could pop them out between takes. Bryce Soderberg played the character in Vancouver, and then Luca Hayes played him in Dubai.

Visual effects also gave him a digital blink, which allowed us to spread the eyes further apart and not have to conform to the anatomy of the human face as much. It was an easy thing to do on their part, but it instantly gave life to an open, unblinking eye.

LENNIE MACDONALD: I think Satine was actually played by three different actors. One time it was Bryce, who was going out with Joel's daughter-in-law, and he played it quite a bit. And when we went to Dubai, the costumer's son Luca was wearing it. I made at least three different rigs for them, each of which was customized to the actor wearing it.

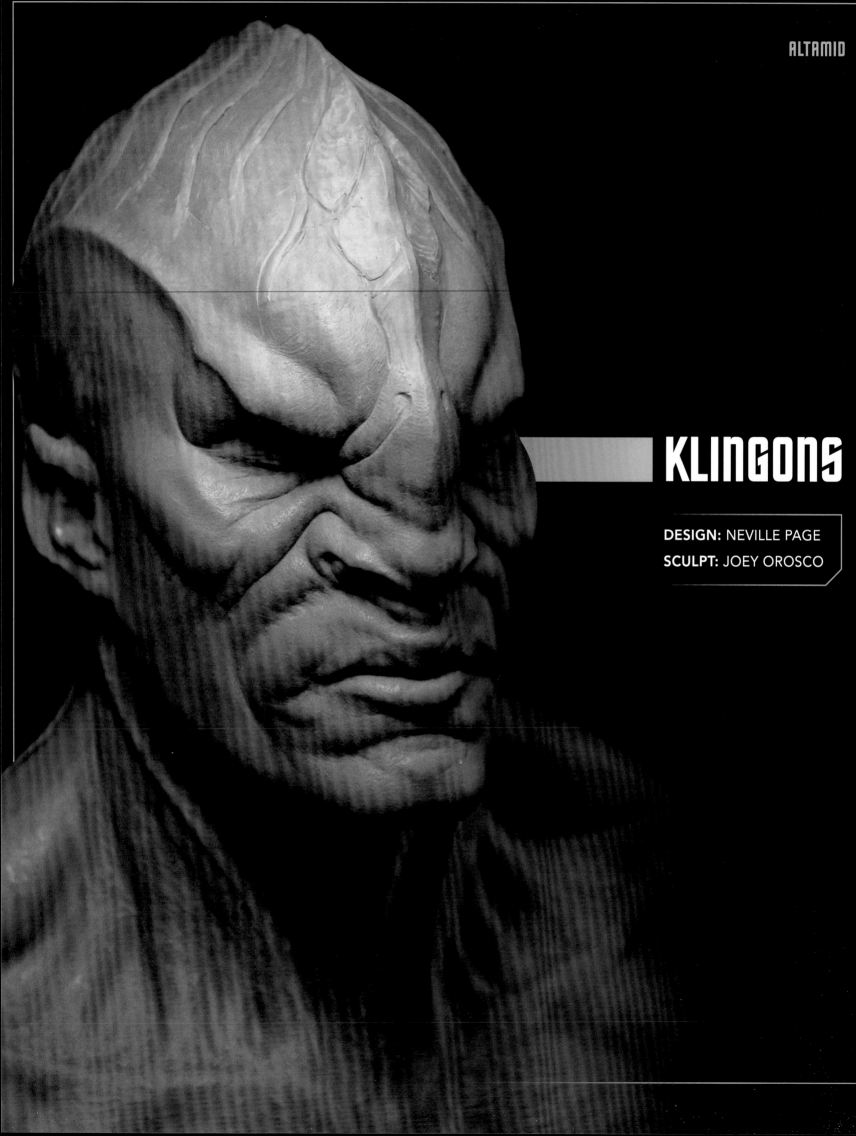

KLINGONS

DESIGN: NEVILLE PAGE
SCULPT: JOEY OROSCO

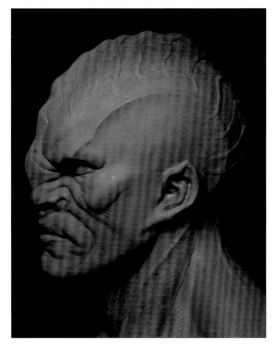

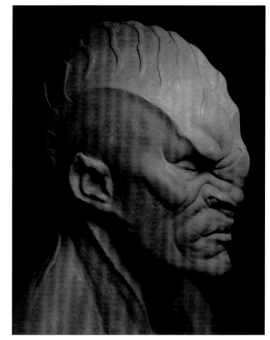

ABOVE: Neville Page's Z-Brush designs for the never-used Klingon.

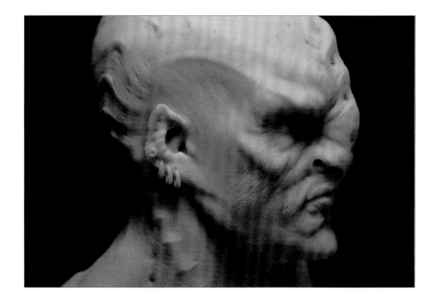

As I mentioned in an earlier chapter, there were going to be Klingons in the 2009 film, but unfortunately the scene they were in was left on the cutting-room floor. As it turns out, there was going to be a Klingon in *Beyond*. Initially, one of the three scavengers in that first encounter with Jaylah was going to be a Klingon. Based on one of Neville Page's designs, Joey Orosco sculpted an initial Klingon makeup, but after the script was changed that design was never molded or cast. We kept trying to get him into the film but, alas, the sculpture never made it to the molding process.

ABOVE: Joey Orosco's Klingon sculpture, based on a Neville Page design.

TEENAXI

DESIGN & SCULPT:
JOEY OROSCO

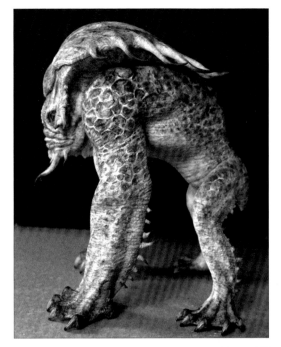

ABOVE: Joey Orosco's finished Teenaxi maquette was used by visual FX to create the digital version of the creatures.

The original concept for the aliens in the opening sequence was a crab shell that appears very benign when you are looking at it, and then its head flips up and you see these angry mandibles when it's in attack mode. There are still some remnants of that idea, although the 'pleasant face' concept doesn't really play in the prologue as it exists now.

Neville Page had done a number of designs, which Justin really liked, but when the prologue was pushed further down the line we didn't have to jump on building those characters until later. During this period, the concept was changed and so Joey Orosco designed three or four new versions, some with prominent shells and others with tentacles. Justin liked one that Joey had rendered with the new concept in mind, so Joey sculpted it and Lance Webb added a truly fantastic paint job.

We created a fully finished maquette that was scanned by the visual-effects department. It was basically a one-to-one scale maquette that matched the scale they are in the film. Ron Ames, the visual-effects supervisor/producer, scanned and animated it. For a later scene, the wardrobe department made a little blue Starfleet shirt for it, so we put that on and scanned again for the end sequence at Kirk's birthday party. Initially we were going to make a full-size costume that a performer could've worn and then get digitally reduced in size, but we were doing so much already that it just wasn't practical to go to those lengths when this option was available to us.

RIGHT: Early Joey Orosco concept drawings of the Teenaxi.

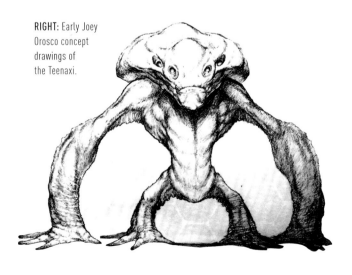

NATALIA

DESIGN: ALLEN WILLIAMS
AND DON LANNING

SCULPT: JOEY OROSCO

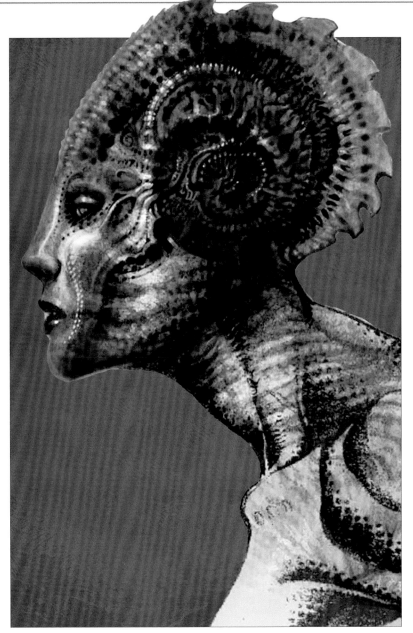

ABOVE: Very early Natalia concept designs suggest the grace and beauty of the final character.

atalia began life as an Allen Williams/Don Lanning crossover. The details and refinements are Allen's, but the Nautilus concept was both Allen's and Don's. I think it was Allen's first, but the width and size of the shell in his initial design wasn't as large as it wound up being. Don's contribution was a small maquette that was very rough, but had the mass to the shell that we ultimately went with, so we took the mass and the size of the head shell from Don's maquette and translated the details of Allen's renderings on top. Actually, I think it was a photo of Don's maquette that I sent to Allen, who did the illustration that ultimately came back. In the hands of Joey Orosco, who was arguably my lead sculptor on the film, the character really took off. Joey

brought his own sensibilities to it and really made it work; he basically gave it the life that you see on film.

It was only when Joey started sculpting the head that I wanted to expand the look of the character beyond a head and hands. I wanted to show as much alien anatomy as we could and really push the envelope. The entire shop was very enthusiastic about this character, so that's why you now see the arms and the back part of the chest. Joey and I have a great working relationship that normally consists of me saying, 'How about this?' and him taking that idea and delivering something better than I ever thought it could be.

When Jeffrey Chernov brought me on to the film, I suggested the character of Natalia and told him

ABOVE: Early Natalia concept designs by Allen Williams.

RIGHT: Don Lanning's rough Natalia maquette.

what I was planning on doing with the makeup, how extreme it was going to be, and that it was going to require somebody that was not going to complain and who would embrace the character. Ashley Edner, my stepdaughter, has sat for makeups with me many times before, so I knew that she had the fortitude and could take the potential limitations of the gigantic shell while still delivering a great performance in the makeup and would be happy to do it, so that was an easy decision. What it did require, since Joey had already sculpted the face and head generically, was to cast the head (shell) piece, put it on Ashley's life cast and then re-cast Ashley's head so we could sculpt the face specifically for her. Gil Laberto, my mold shop foreman, found an incredibly lightweight and super-durable material. You

could take that head and throw it against the wall and nothing would happen to it, it was extremely tough. It was basically just a hollow shell, so that made it incredibly lightweight.

We were two days before our last day of filming and still hadn't put Natalia on camera. We had just finished working all day and since this character was never scripted, there had been some question as to what sequence Natalia would be in. We obviously wanted her to be very prominent in whatever sequence it was; even though she was a background character, I wanted to push her as far to the foreground as possible.

It was finally determined, with just a couple of days left, that the best place to put her was Kirk's surprise birthday party. It was ten in the evening when the

DON LANNING: That Nautilus shape has been running around Hollywood for the last 40 years, but it's one of those wonderful categories where you haven't experienced the archetype yet. My understanding is that Joel took a simple maquette that I had done in a couple of hours and sent it on to Allen, who redrew it as female with a strong bridge to the nose and with a smaller shell, and then Joey Orosco got hold of it and made it even more wonderful to look at.

RIGHT: Joey Orosco's Natalia sculpture.

decision was made: we'll put her in the birthday party. The other option was the massive starship dock in Yorktown on the last day of filming, where we had the majority of our aliens working, but I knew she would get lost in it.

So it then became a question of, 'Okay, do we forgo sleep and jump into this seven-hour makeup application to get it on film in a more prominent scene, or do we take our turnaround time, come in and put it off until the last day and just have her be one of the many characters

ABOVE: The Natalia makeup was applied by Harlow, Werner Pretorius, Steve Buscaino and Lennie MacDonald.

in that sequence?' After spending months and months creating this character, pre-painting and testing it, we knew what the right decision was. There was no way I was going to allow myself to be sitting in the theater thinking, 'If I had only stayed up…' I think I got half an hour's sleep and jumped right into it. That sequence was the right place to put her, and we put her in a cocktail dress so you could see her arms and back, so it made sense all around.

I should also talk about the pre-painting on the character, which was done by an incredible Vancouver artist named Bronwyne Sloley, who basically designed and replicated that paint job. As brilliant as the original sculpture was, the paintwork on her is equally as stunning and compliments the shapes and details brilliantly. Joey and Bronwyne's artistic eyes really came together on Natalia. Since Joey was with me in Vancouver, he had some input into what the paint job should be, as did I. Even though we were shooting, I would come in with my ideas for the shell, and what I wanted the skin tones and patterns to be. But Bronwyne definitely deserves all the recognition for that paintwork.

The makeup was applied by myself, Werner Pretorius, Lennie MacDonald and Steve Buscaino, all coming together for the application of that character. The eyes were done by Cristina Patterson and the teeth were by Toby Lindala, so it's fair to say a lot of people had a hand in that character.

JOEY OROSCO: As far as everything I've created, even compared to things like the Triceratops in *Jurassic Park* and all the great things I did on *Avatar*, this was one of the best creations I've ever been a part of. It was so amazing to be a part of creating Natalia, that beautiful shell head and a beautiful makeup. It's iconic now, and is going to be iconic forever. I chose Bronwyn to paint the piece, who's a beautiful painter.

When that design was given to me, Joel said, 'Go for it!' so I started looking at nature and seashells. Not to take anything away from Don Lanning, but I literally took it in my own heart and designed something out of my brain, from a rough, *rough* concept that Don Lanning did. I made it happen with Joel Harlow's great direction, and what you see in the film is my own concept and my own thoughts with Joel Harlow's art direction, so that's how it ended up. I'm the man who sculpted the actual makeup and nobody [else] can take the credit for that.

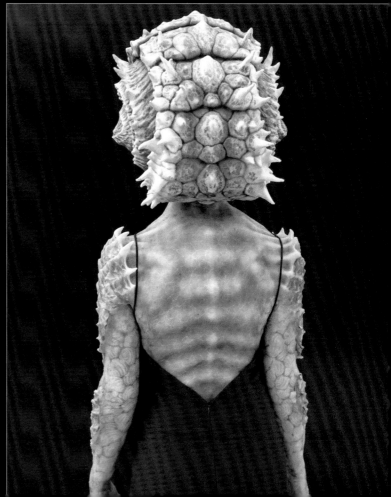

ELEPHANT SLUG

DESIGN: ALLEN WILLIAMS (HEAD); DON LANNING AND JOEL HARLOW (BODY)

SCULPT: NORMAN CABRERA (HEAD); DON LANNING (BODY)

P7.34D.0.0.1

The Elephant Slug has a long, convoluted history. It started off as an unused design for an alternate prologue sequence. This character was going to be a 'humanoid' alien ambassador to what eventually became the Teenaxi. We had big plans for it, including animating the tentacles on its elaborate head. Tim Ralston, who did our mechanics, was going to give us a bounty of tentacle movement via servo. When that initial concept went away, Norman Cabrera had already finished the sculpture of the head, based on an Allen Williams design.

I knew I wanted to put it in somewhere in the film because it was too good to go unused. I pushed to get it molded, so at least the Wed clay sculpture would not fall to dust. Once secure in a mold, it sat dormant until we were in Vancouver and could revive it in another form.

BELOW: Side view of unpainted Elephant Slug head sculpture.

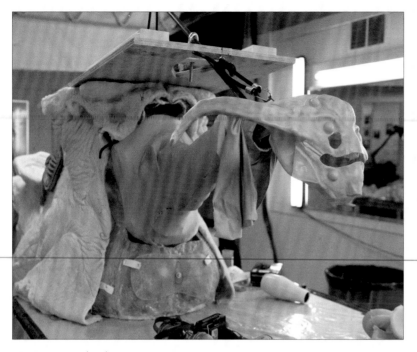

ABOVE: Bryan Blair (right) oversees the massive Elephant Slug puppeteering elements.

At that point, producer Lindsey Weber came to me and said that J.J. wanted to see something non-humanoid, so this seemed like the perfect opportunity to bring back this character, or at least its head. I flew Don Lanning up from Los Angeles so he could sculpt a suitable alien body for Norman's already-finished head sculpture. My concept behind the entire character was a kind of alien 'pack mule', carrying around its owner's luggage. I figured that having a large box on the creature's back would easily give us the ability to hide puppeteers inside, allowing us to get very broad stroke movements from the puppet.

Gil Laberto and John Halfman molded the character at lightning speed. Bryan Blair engineered and puppeteered the whole thing, with the assistance of a performer in the tail. Even though we didn't have mechanics in what were originally the tentacles, we turned them into more of a tentacle/horn element, so it wasn't so obvious that they weren't moving independently. Bryan mechanized the neck and added a breathing rig to the sides of the 'slug'. It had a moving tail, and it could walk. There was one person at the bottom working the legs, the breathing and the tail, and the other person (Bryan) on top would straddle them and work the head and neck.

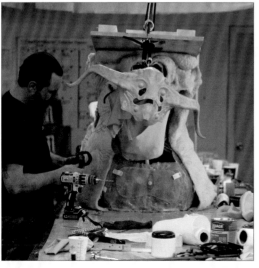

ABOVE: Bryan Blair, Norman Cabrera and Don Lanning work on different elements of the Elephant Slug mold and sculpture.

ALLEN WILLIAMS: If I remember correctly, the character was originally referred to as a doctor. I had sent in a design for a cephalopod kind of creature head that wasn't quite in the Cthulhu realm, but it had a large head with tentacles on the front of the face, and Joel, who's a Lovecraftian at heart, said, 'Come back with an idea for this character'. At one point it was going to be at the very beginning of the movie and they were going to open on that shot, so I thought, 'Okay, Joel really digs the tentacle shapes, so let's do something with that!' My idea was that if this character was going to talk, its mouth would expand impossibly hugely and extend down the length of its tentacles, so I guess you could say it was an homage to our love of the Lovecraftian aesthetic.

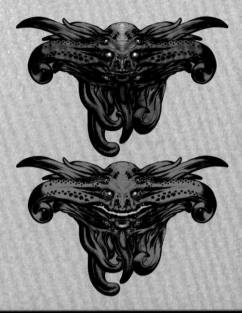

DON LANNING: Even though the character was cut from the original opening, we wanted to find a place for that head, which had a wonderful character to it. I flew out to Vancouver and sculpted the body in ten days, putting a lot of detail into it like a saddle and wrinkles, and it became a really interesting creature. It had some nice tail movement as it moved along the floor on its belly, with these giant arthritic hands holding on to that box. I think it's the closest thing we've had to a *Star Wars* character in the *Star Trek* universe. The design aesthetic of *Star Trek* was always humanoid, not necessarily anything animatronic, but it felt right to finally do an animatronic character and I'm glad we got to do it.

"J.J. WANTED TO SEE SOMETHING NON-HUMANOID, SO THIS SEEMED LIKE THE PERFECT OPPORTUNITY TO BRING BACK THIS CHARACTER, OR AT LEAST ITS HEAD."

Joel on the Elephant Slug's return to the movie, after its original humanoid incarnation had been dropped

ABOVE: Close-ups of the Elephant Slug's arm and head.

VULCANS

SCULPT (EARS): JOEL HARLOW AND RICHIE ALONZO

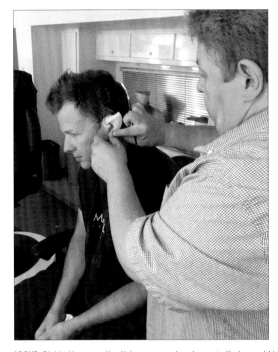  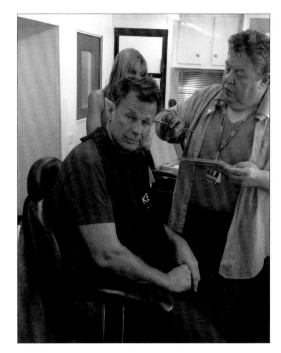

ABOVE: Richie Alonzo applies Vulcan ears and eyebrows to Harlow and his (Harlow's) wife, Cindy.

There are a few Vulcans in the film. Aside from Spock, the most notable are the Vulcan ambassadors that deliver the news of Spock Prime's passing. Actually, my wife Cindy and I donned the Vulcan ears, hair, and brows for a sequence we filmed in Dubai. It wasn't the first time I oversaw the department and appeared in makeup—I did the same thing on *The Lone Ranger* a few years ago. With *Star Trek Beyond*, I knew I wanted to be in there somewhere. Initially I was going to be a character covered in makeup, but there was no time for that. There was too much to do, so I thought it would be nice to play a Vulcan. Sanja Hays, the costume designer, was behind the idea and so was Justin, the director. We were able to slot ourselves in during the last days we were shooting in Dubai. I don't think we're in the film, but at least there are photos of it to remember it by.

I was also doing Zachary Quinto's Spock makeup every day along with Felix Fox, so I certainly felt it was

 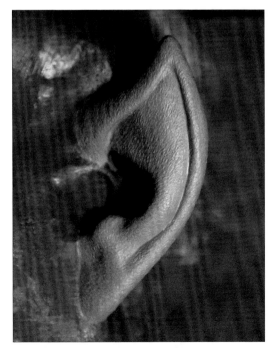 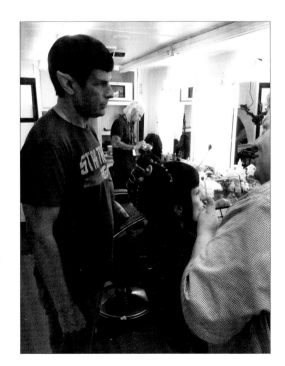

ABOVE: Alonzo applies Cindy Harlow's Vulcan makeup while her husband (note the *Star Trek* t-shirt) looks on. Center: Vulcan ear close-up.

RICHIE ALONZO: I remember putting Joel's ears on him, and before finishing his makeup he had to finish somebody else's makeup he was involved with, so Felix and I started putting Cindy's ears on her. When she didn't want to pluck her eyebrows, I said, 'I've got an idea!' Luckily her eyebrows were fine enough that I could glue them flat and cover the portion I needed to cover with a Bondo Pros-Aide cream. It covered and camouflaged part of her eyebrows, so I just had to extend them by laying on hair to extend the edge of the eyebrow and give her that Vulcan look. She was really grateful for that, and I think I did it on Joel too just to make it look like they'd shaved the ends of their eyebrows.

Doing that to Zach every day would have been totally out of the question because he has eyebrows enough for five people! His eyebrows are so full and thick that we were going to start tweezing them into shape, so we gave him a mirror, but he said, 'Just tell me what I need to pull out!' so he started tweezing his own eyebrows to thin them out a bit and we shaved off the tail end, so he was a real trouper about it. And every day, Joel would apply the individual hairs to create the tail end of those Vulcan eyebrows.

RIGHT: Joel and Cindy Harlow make their *Star Trek* debut as Vulcans.

more appropriate to be part of that Vulcan lineage than burying myself in a 'random alien number six' makeup. I also wanted to be recognizable with my wife on film, even though we didn't make it in. I remember we were in Dubai and I had my makeup on. Zack was not working that day, but he came by for a haircut. He looked over at me because I had the wig on and was in full makeup, and I kind of looked like him from a distance and Zack told me that I could have easily been his double.

With the Vulcan ears there's no margin for error. They need to be treated as a subtle, realistic makeup. With an alien like Natalia or one of our background aliens you can get away with certain things, but when you are dealing with human flesh tones and human anatomy (for the most part), there's really no disguising it if it goes south on you. Even though this is the third movie with Zack as Spock, you never want to adopt the attitude of 'Oh, we got this, let's focus on something else!' because they could end up biting you in a big way. We wanted to make everything better that we had done previously, so Richie re-sculpted two new versions of the ears and we tested both of them. Between Zack, myself, Justin and production, we picked the set we felt was the best and that's what we went with.

DEEP C-ZER

DESIGN: DON LANNING
AND JOEL HARLOW

SCULPT: DON LANNING

ABOVE: Side, front and back views of Werner Pretorius' alternate Deep C-Zer sculpture.

This character was initially going to be the female Keenser (played by Deep Roy), a potential love interest. We started calling her 'Queenser' in the shop. When the script got rewritten, we still had this great sculpture that Don had done. We had already molded the back of the head piece, so it was an easy decision to sculpt a new face rather than keeping a Keenser type of face, and turn it into a new character.

Because of my love for the ocean, I started pushing Don toward doing something more aquatic, using a catfish type of mouth anatomy. Lennie MacDonald painted the finished makeup with a special color-shifting powder, which made it very otherworldly. It primarily looked like copper or brass, but if it turned in any direction it suddenly shifted colors to blue and then green.

BELOW: Different versions of Don Lanning's Deep C-Zer show the character's original similarity to Keenser.

ABOVE: The Deep C-Zer makeup utilized a color-shifting reflective paint scheme designed by Lennie MacDonald.

DON LANNING: My understanding was that somewhere in the bar sequence Keenser was going to meet his mate, but that got changed or dropped. I had done this beautiful sculpture of a specific character, so what we did was keep the cowl and this beautiful fishlike carapace, and retrofit a fishier face on it and create another workable character that was still beautiful. You can see Joel's art direction in the corners of the mouth and a bit of a hanging tendril there, while the multiple nostrils and the angles of the eyes were mine. That headpiece was so beautiful it didn't make sense to throw it away, so we were able to redo the face and come up with something new.

Lennie came over to my desk one day and said, 'I'm going to use a special color-shifting paint that the government uses for money. I've got to sign some paperwork and get approved for its use, because they want to know what I'm using it for'. So he went and got that weird paint, which is not holographic, but it shifts color, although I don't think it was really showcased in the film.

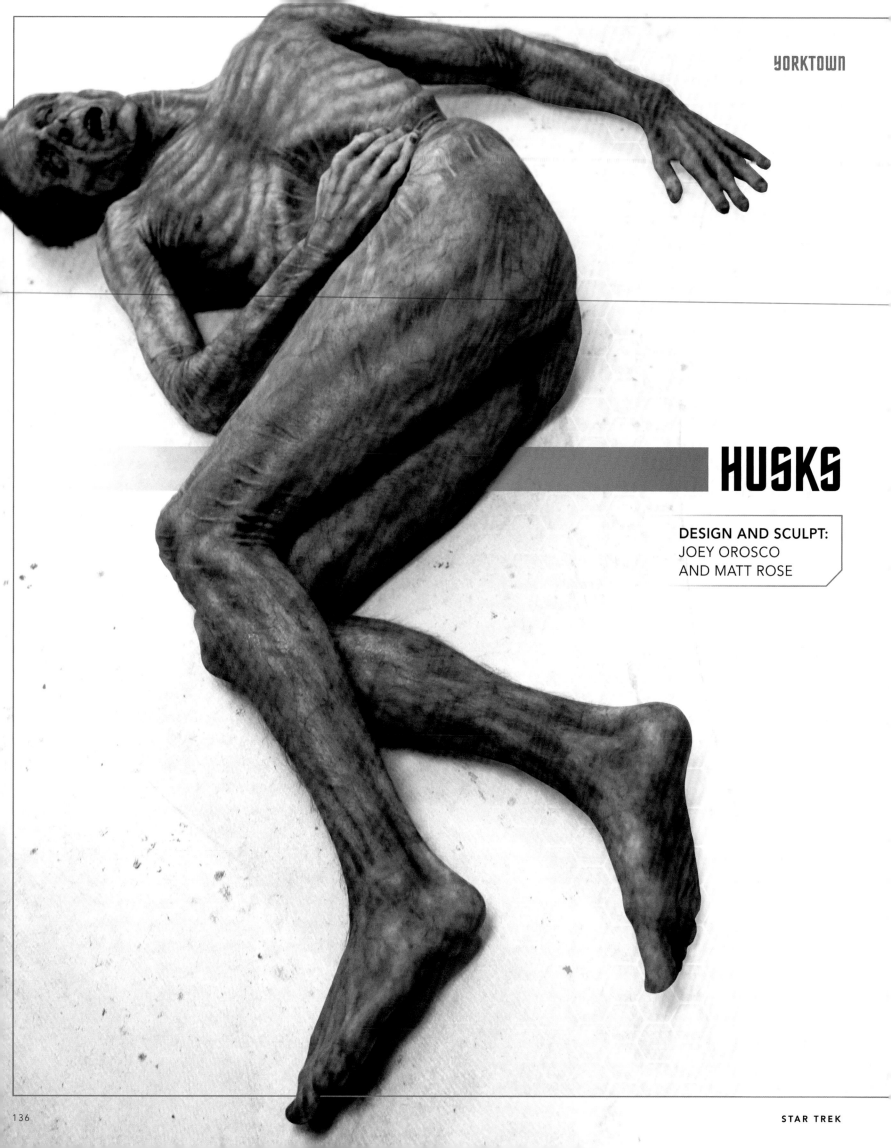

HUSKS

DESIGN AND SCULPT:
JOEY OROSCO
AND MATT ROSE

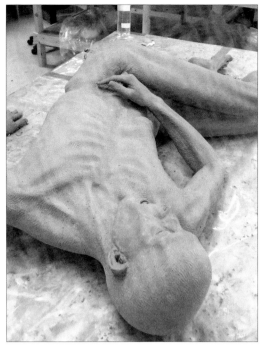
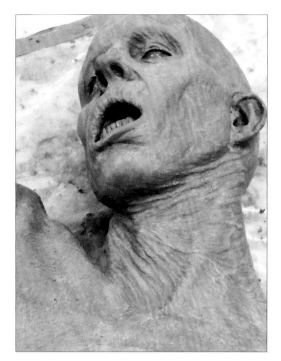

ABOVE: Matt Rose (right) sculpts one of the various drained 'husks.'

Matt Rose created three replacement heads for a sequence in which the character of 'Cupcake' gets drained of his genetic essence by 'stage one' Krall. Cupcake is the character you see in the first film at the bar where Kirk and Uhura meet. He is the crewman that interferes in Kirk's attempt to 'pick-up' Uhura, eliciting Kirk's response of 'Hey, take it easy, Cupcake!' He was originally Krall's first victim from the *Enterprise* crew, and you see him get drained of life in front of everybody. We built three different heads that we would replace in stages as he got more and more emaciated.

Initially, Matt did something a bit more real looking, more like a 'bog-man' feel, but Justin wanted a more exaggerated, 1980s horror head, which is what we ultimately went with. There are a few more victims of Krall's DNA-draining process throughout the film, the biggest being a piece that Joey Orosco sculpted. This corpse was a nude full body that the crew finds towards the end of the film. They put two and two together, realizing that Krall is not going to look like he did during their last confrontation. He's going to look more human now, because they come across this 6'2" Starfleet captain drained of his life force. That's when they know they're looking for somebody that doesn't look like the stage 3 or 4 version of Krall. We took Bryce Soderberg, who played the first Satine character in Vancouver, and did a body cast of him. We cast the body in clay so Joey could sculpt it down to a desiccated corpse.

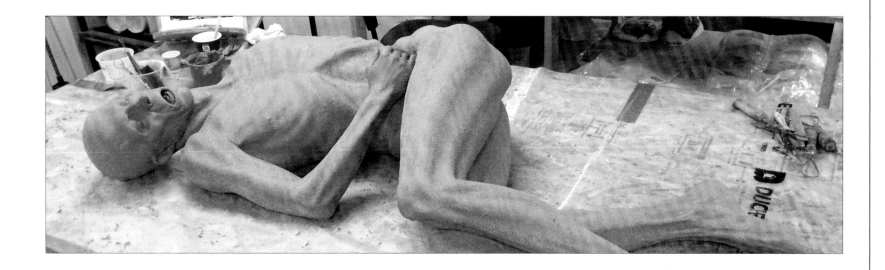

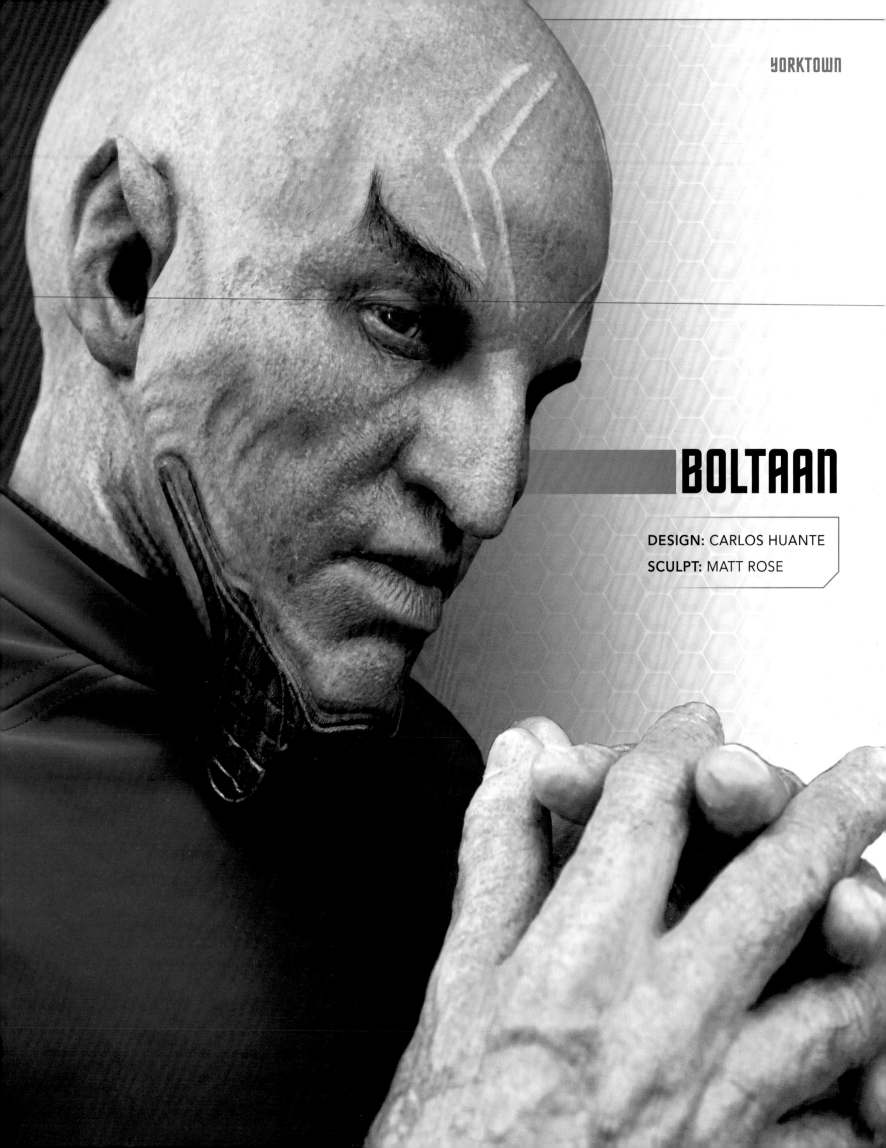

BOLTAAN

DESIGN: CARLOS HUANTE
SCULPT: MATT ROSE

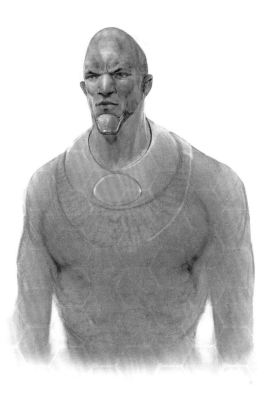

Every inch of this character is covered with prosthetics. Carlos Huante did the concept illustration as part of the initial concept for the original version of the film. It was a concept for what would have been our main villain. When Justin came aboard, he gravitated toward the look of that design, so we repurposed it as one of our peripheral alien characters. The makeup itself was sculpted by Matt Rose.

When I did the test application for Boltaan we had him dressed in a Starfleet science officer uniform, though the regal look of his chin and brows don't really fit with a typical Starfleet uniform. He has an ornamental chin piece, which was part of the original concept and gave him an Egyptian Pharaoh look. I liked that test application better than the day we actually applied him for the film, where he was to be seen in Yorktown base. You actually get to see a good bit of him in the film—he gets into a teleporter and hits a couple of buttons, swirling lights appear around him and he's teleported somewhere.

We actually applied that makeup on Werner Pretorius, one of my key makeup artists on the film. That scene was shot in Dubai, but we tested it back in Vancouver on a different actor. Werner was coming with us so, much to his reluctance, we assigned the look to be played by him.

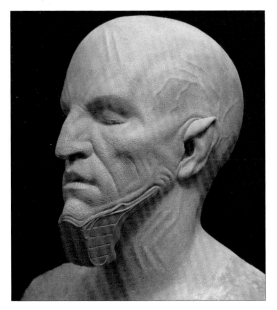
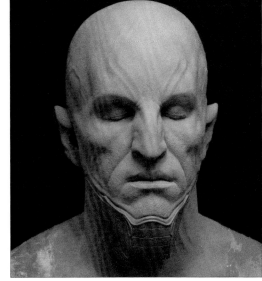
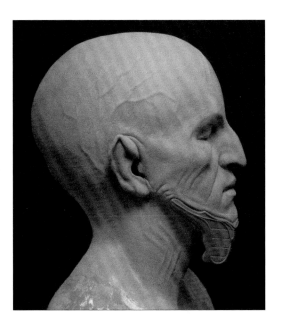

ABOVE: Matt Rose's Boltaan sculpture.

ABOVE: Harlow and Richie Alonzo apply the Boltaan makeup.

"IT WAS A CONCEPT FOR WHAT WOULD HAVE BEEN OUR MAIN VILLAIN. WHEN JUSTIN CAME ABOARD HE GRAVITATED TOWARD THE LOOK OF THAT DESIGN, SO WE REPURPOSED IT AS ONE OF OUR PERIPHERAL ALIEN CHARACTERS."

Joel on Boltaan's reduced role in the film

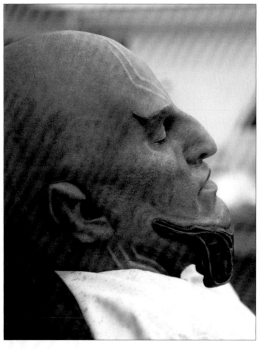

ABOVE: Applying the Boltaan makeup to makeup artist Werner Pretorius (note Harlow's Vulcan ears in readiness for his upcoming cameo).

CLASSIC ALIEN

DESIGN AND SCULPT:

DON LANNING

ABOVE: Don Lanning's original sculpture is loosely based on a character from the 2009 film.

That character was designed and sculpted by Don Lanning as a background character, and I believe we did three versions of background masks, with each one painted by different people. That was the cool thing about these background masks: I had so many great painters to choose from that you could give the same mask to three different people and get three different, unique-looking aliens, even though they came from the same sculpture.

When Don and I began talking about this alien, we referenced a character in the first *Star Trek* film in the scene when Kirk is born. There is a nurse, played by an actress with digital augmentation to spread her eyes further apart. This character started out as a version of that nurse, but then it evolved into more of a classic gray alien. I remember having multiple conversations about that character on the first film, so I guess some of it stuck with me and we tried to revive it here in some small way.

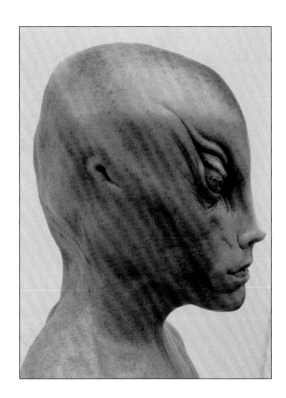

ABOVE: The final painted 'classic alien'; one of several versions in the film.

ABOVE: A different wardrobe and paint job creates a second 'classic alien'.

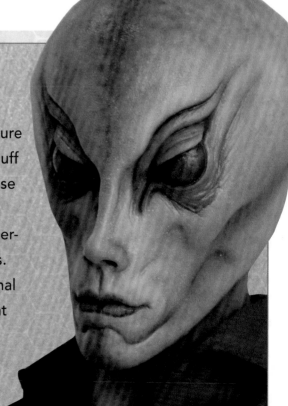

DON LANNING: I remember being surrounded by some of the greatest sculptors in the business at the time, so Joey Orosco was working on the Nautilus girl, Norman Cabrera was working on the most beautiful little creature I've ever seen, Miles Teves was at one elbow, and the new guys had great stuff going. Everybody was sculpting a giant head and I'm thinking, 'My God, these heads are huge!' so this character came out of grabbing an actor's head and doing something different. I wanted to go in the opposite direction and under-sculpt a character with no lines, no wrinkles, just the briefest of explanations. At the same time, I was also looking at an old image of Balok from the original series, which was the dummy representing the Clint Howard character in that episode, so this was also a tip of the hat to the old show.

RIGHT: The 'classic alien', Don Lanning's subtle homage to the original *Star Trek* series.

SHLERM

DESIGN: CARLOS HUANTE
SCULPT: MIKE ROTELLA

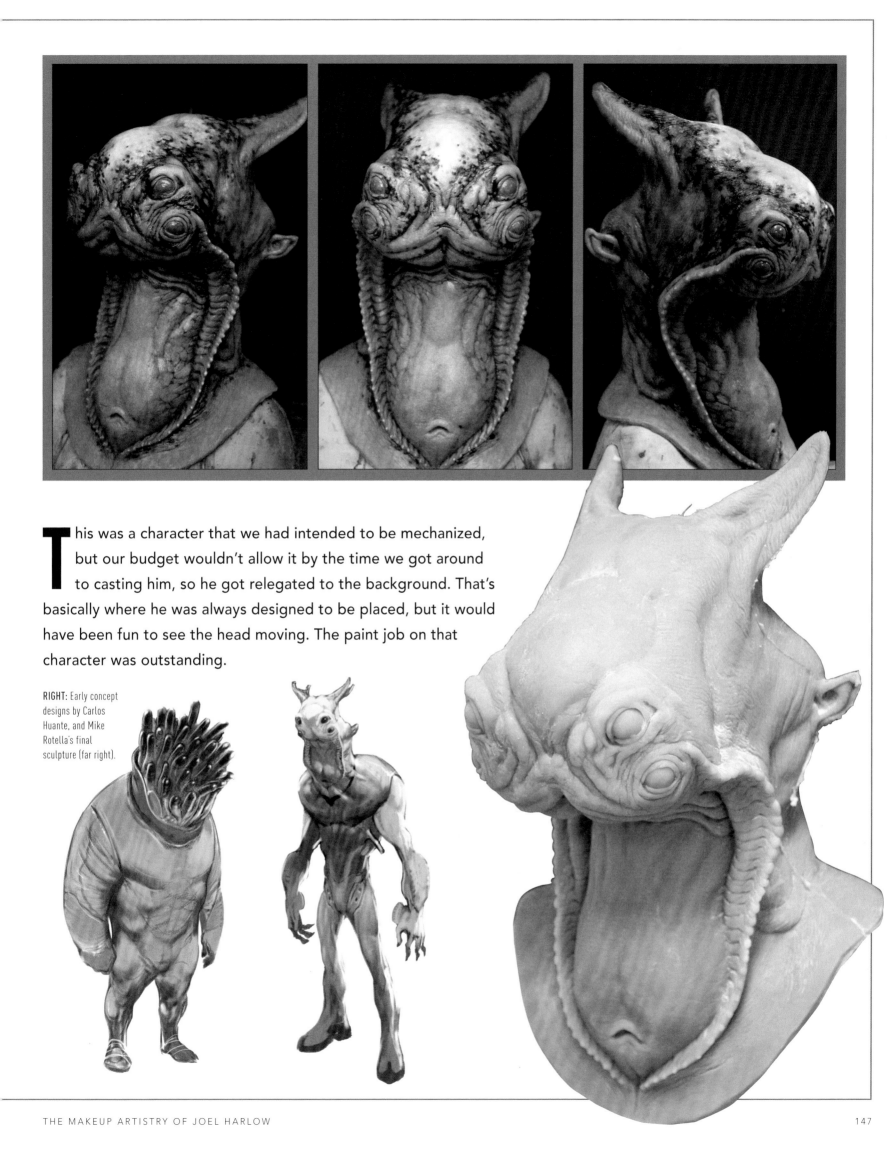

This was a character that we had intended to be mechanized, but our budget wouldn't allow it by the time we got around to casting him, so he got relegated to the background. That's basically where he was always designed to be placed, but it would have been fun to see the head moving. The paint job on that character was outstanding.

RIGHT: Early concept designs by Carlos Huante, and Mike Rotella's final sculpture (far right).

"SHLERM DIDN'T HAVE A HUMANOID VIBE; HE WAS MORE OF A THROWBACK TO THE HAMMERHEAD GUY FROM THE CANTINA IN *STAR WARS*."

Mike Rotella

ABOVE: Finished Shlerm in wardrobe. **RIGHT:** Shlerm's hands were sculpted by Marc Opdycke.

ABOVE: A second Shlerm uses the same sculpture but a different color palette and wardrobe.

Our team in Vancouver did some outstanding paintwork. I hadn't really worked up there since I did *The Outer Limits* TV series with Steve Johnson, so I really relied on Werner Pretorius and Toby Lindala, who reached out to a bunch of artists on my behalf. We brought all of them on board and they turned out to be spectacular. We really seemed to have got the cream of the crop, much to the upset of some of the other studios in Vancouver. We treated everybody with the greatest respect and gave them a bunch of rewarding, creative characters to finish. Everybody bent over backwards, even though we needed to work a lot of long hours and six/seven-day work weeks to get everything done. Everybody was very enthusiastic.

MIKE ROTELLA: I picked up another Carlos Huante character from the stack of designs we had, because I think he's one of the greatest. Although he was eventually named Shlerm, I always thought of him as 'the Slug Lord.' Shlerm didn't have a humanoid vibe; he was more of a throwback to the Hammerhead guy from the cantina in *Star Wars*, so he was really out there design-wise. The funny thing is, I'm sure it took Carlos five minutes to do that little sketch, but all the information was there so you just hope you'll be able to translate it all the way through.

Mark Opdycke made the hands for Shlerm. I think they were originally made for another character, but the sculptures were intact so we took what Mark had started and added stuff to them based on the textures of the head. It was great to see the photos Joel was sending people from set so you could see what they finally looked like. We talked about it all the time, that there was a real heavy *Star Wars* cantina vibe to a lot of stuff we were doing. There's always been a line between the feel of the *Star Wars* universe and *Star Trek*, so it was cool to bridge the gap a little bit.

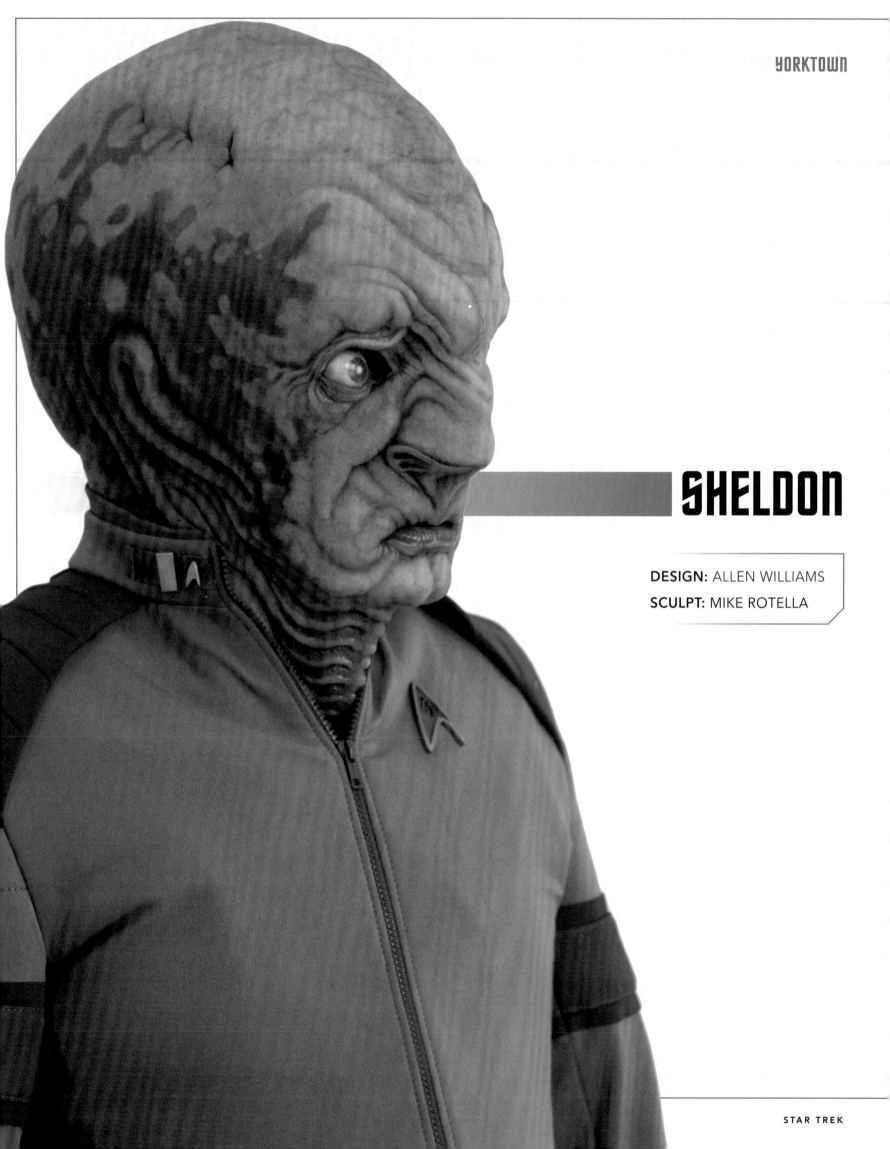

SHELDON

DESIGN: ALLEN WILLIAMS
SCULPT: MIKE ROTELLA

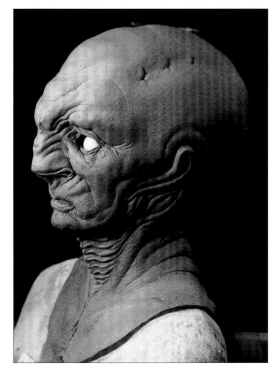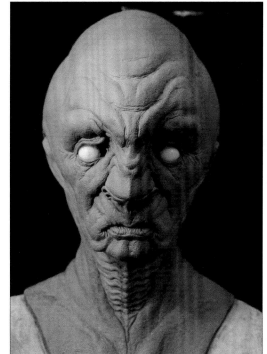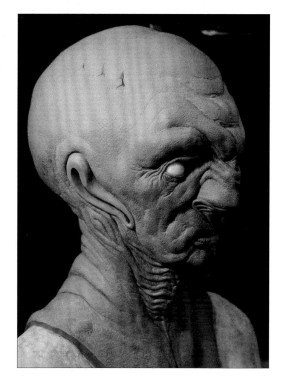

ABOVE: Some different angles of Mike Rotella's Sheldon sculpture.

He was originally an Allen Williams design intended to be a background alien seen in one of Krall's holding cells. I named him Sheldon (not very otherworldly, I know) because he reminded me of my old landlord from my last storage unit—he used to come around all the time when we were there; the second we got there, he would come in five minutes later and wouldn't leave.

At that point in the process, production really trusted what we were doing, so having a completely fleshed-out design wasn't necessary because some of those structures are going to change anyway in the translation to 'camera-ready' makeup. You can have the most beautifully rendered two-dimensional design, but the second you start translating it into a three-dimensional sculpture it begins to change. And in the case of Sheldon, Mike Rotella brought his touch to it and suddenly you had a fun, interesting character with a lot of personality.

ALLEN WILLIAMS: You might see that guy sitting on a pier somewhere fishing. He looks like he could have just been sitting there reading a book in the background somewhere. When I was doing that design, I remember thinking it would be kind of cool to have a character with the demeanor of an old guy. He's an older creature in the universe and very thin, but I thought of him as a knowledgeable, wizened creature who's not very warlike and if you saw him, he was somehow in this moment of peace, and I think he comes across that way. I wanted him to be not as in-your-face as everyone else because it's those little details that sometimes pop out.

I kind of styled him with an ageing, decrepit kind of body to give that bit of frailty, but there's also an alien aspect to him because you don't know what his physiology is so you don't know if that frailty is believable. We've come to see aliens and creatures with their different physiologies and you can have something that is very thin also be very strong, so you don't really know if he's as peaceful and vulnerable as he appears to be.

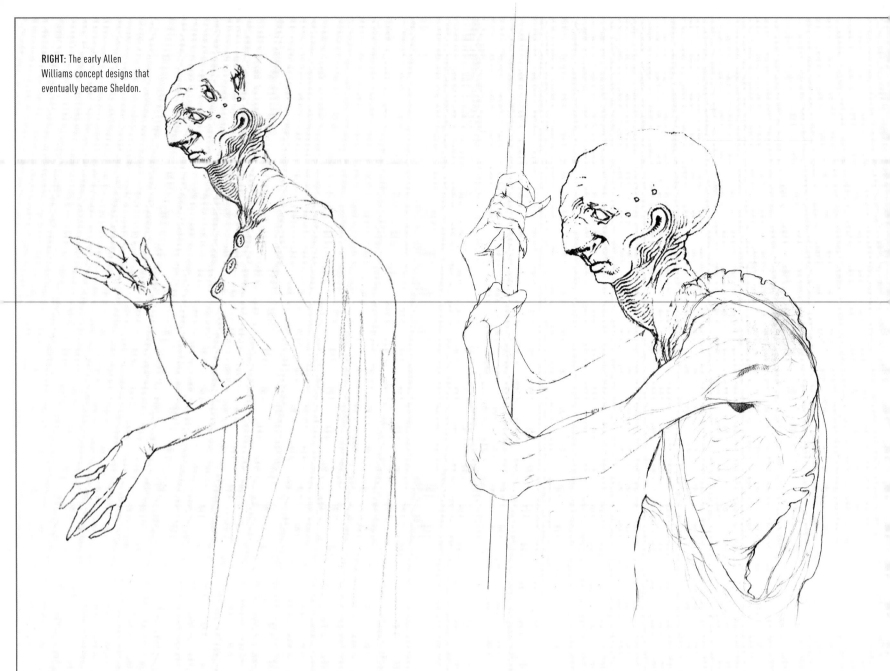

MIKE ROTELLA: The first character I got to do on my own as a full-head sculpture was affectionately known as Sheldon. Allen Williams did a quick sketch, like a profile shot, but it was so cool I asked if I could try that one and Joel said, 'Yeah, go for it!' I started roughing it out and after a few hours he came by and said, 'You're actually pretty good at this!' I think that's when he thought, 'This guy can handle this stuff'.

The best part of Allen's original sketch is the fact that it's so quick, but Allen still manages to nail this really interesting character. It wasn't as detailed as some of his other stuff, so I could play with it a bit. With so many Z-Brush designs today, you get 3D turnarounds so you're pretty much just making that character. But when you can say, 'This is a really quick and interesting sketch!' and you have to figure out how to realize it in three dimensions, that's the most fun you can have as a sculptor because you're able to put a bit of your own spin on it. Maybe it looks like he's got a couple of different nostrils or some gills on the side, so you get to mess around with those things.

That sketch was a profile with a really nice shape to it, so my first job was to get the overall shape and then start to whittle it down. If there's something specific not in that sketch, like skin texture or wrinkles, you just add that stuff as you go along. Maybe you'll say to yourself, 'His skin looks like an old man living in the desert', and you'll then incorporate those little wrinkles in the design. And sometimes those seemingly random, accidental swirly pencil marks actually suggest something that you will put into your sculpture, so it becomes an important design element.

CRABBIE

DESIGN: DON LANNING (HEAD)
MILES TEVES (BODY—UNUSED)

SCULPT: DON LANNING

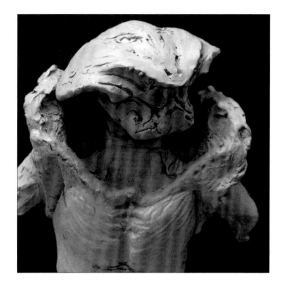

ABOVE: Early Don Lanning 'crab' sculptures, when the characters were to be seen in the film's prologue sequence.

As I discussed earlier, we were originally working on characters for the prologue sequence, where the little creatures you see now were going to be these crab-like creatures. Don Lanning sculpted the head element of those original Teenaxi aliens, which Justin really liked, and we were going to translate the rest of that anatomy onto the body for that sequence. I had Miles Teves render a couple of designs for that look to give Justin a sense of what the bodies could look like.

Ultimately we postponed the build on that part of it, which was now going to be shot much later in the schedule, and we began focusing on other characters. When we finally circled back to it, Joey had done four or five designs of different versions of these little Teenaxi aliens, which ended up being used instead. But we still had the head and shoulders of Crabbie and we wanted to use every single alien we created in the film, so it was relegated to one of the background characters.

We still needed to complete the look, however, and fortunately I had a huge lobster claw that I had picked up in Massachusetts while working on *Black Mass*. We molded it, cast it in silicone and threw it into a vat of kerosene. When silicone and kerosene meet, the silicone swells to at least twice the original size within a few days, so we now had this gigantic crab claw that we molded and cast rigid parts from, and they became Crabbie's hands.

The original concept for the crab creatures would be the idea that if the actor wearing the head tipped his neck forward, you were basically looking at the top of the head as the 'face'. The markings looked very benign and pleasant, so you were fooled into thinking that this was a passive alien. When he tips his head back, you realize they're just markings on the top of his head, and his real face is horrific and angry as he comes at you with gnashing claws.

DON LANNING: The character started as a lizard creature, with a helmet that dropped down to look like a face, so that shield-like helmet became the face of the character. I blocked out a sculpture, leaving a piece of armature wire in the neck that I could puppeteer, and sure enough we had a couple of show-and-tell meetings where I found myself puppeteering this helmeted head, so that was a lot of fun. My understanding was that Joey Orosco sculpted the final version of a different character, which was a smaller-sized creature we now see in the opening of the movie. We ended up with the other crab character, which was just a head, but I don't think you ever see it.

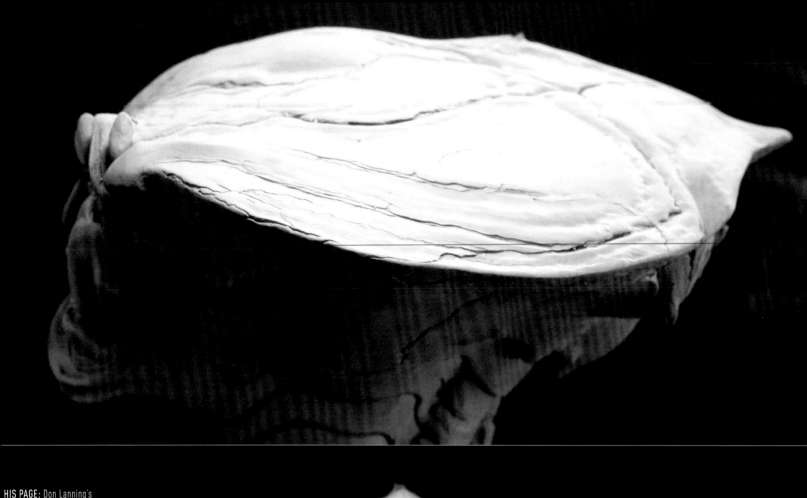

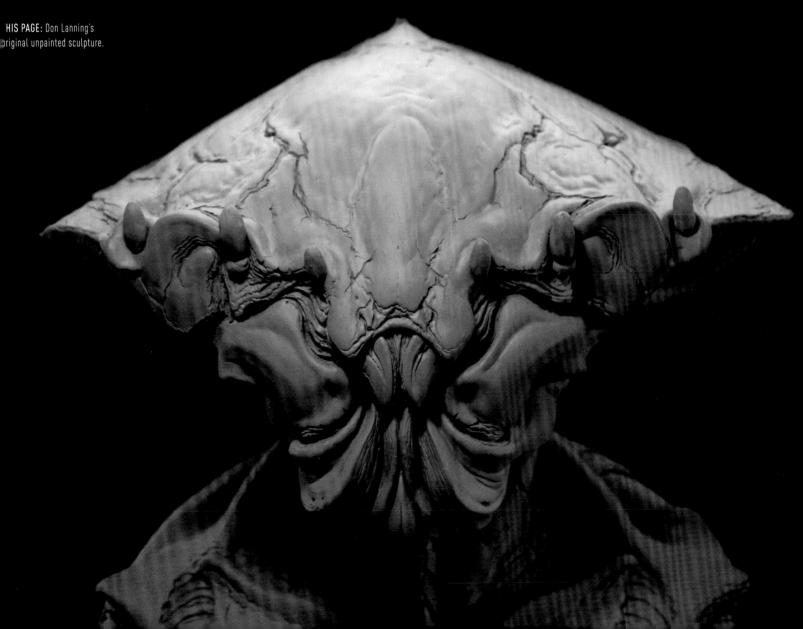

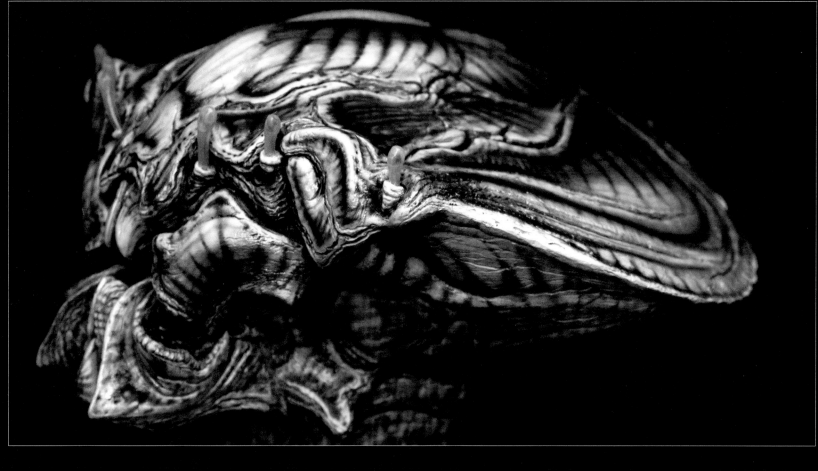

THIS PAGE: The final painted 'Crabbie.'

SIR OLDEN

DESIGN: CARLOS HUANTE
SCULPT: MIKE ROTELLA

This was a Carlos Huante design that translated much differently from what it looked like on paper. We had sculpted it back in Burbank on a generic life cast and though most of the makeups that were approached in this manner were very successful, we had a hard time fitting this on potential performers in Vancouver. Eventually, when we found the right performer, it changed even more and I think it was successful in the long run.

The coloring and finishing on Sir Olden is a good example of letting the sculpture take the lead rather than letting the paintwork overpower the character. Mike Rotella did a great job in sculpting this makeup—it's up to the sculptor to make sure the pieces all fit together and overlap properly but usually, when it comes to a generic makeup, the pieces are inevitably going to have to be adjusted when you apply the makeup. I'm pretty good at making generic prosthetics work on actors, which is one of the reasons I tested all of the alien characters myself.

The 'stone' element in the center of Sir Olden's forehead is a bit ambiguous in the original design. I suppose I pictured it as a piece of metal or a gem, so I had Mike sculpt a different texture on it that we could address with a different finish when we started casting the character in Vancouver.

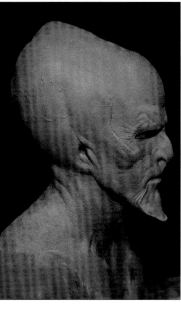
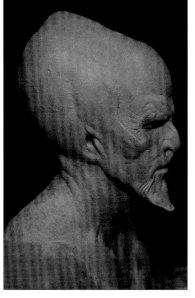
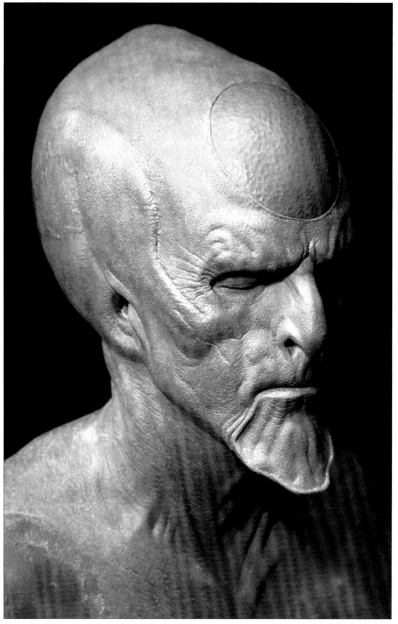

THIS PAGE: Early Carlos Huante concept designs (top);Mike Rotella's final Sir Olden sculpture (above and right).

ABOVE: A slightly different version of Sir Olden including different forehead ˙stone˙.   **RIGHT:** Sir Olden's forehead ˙stone˙ was thought to be a piece of metal or a gem.

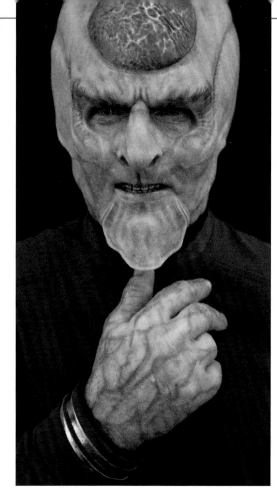

ABOVE: Three views of Sir Olden makeup showcasing the finished forehead 'stone' and hands.

MIKE ROTELLA: I had finished work on Shlerm, so I guess Joel thought I could handle a multi-piece appliance makeup. It's not something I had done many times, but I thought I could handle it. The character came from another minimal sketch by Carlos, but it had a lot of cool stuff going on and a lot of weird information. Norman Cabrera was originally going to do the character, but he was already swamped with work so he handed it off to me, which made it even more intense because it was Norman's guy and now I had to finish it!

That big circle in the forehead was a weird design element. It could have been anything from a painted circle to an actual part of his anatomy, so Joel and I decided it was maybe part of his head that was exposed. I put some wrinkles around it to make it look like protruding skull, and then gave it a hammered bronze or steel look just to add some texture to it. I had this idea that it was some metal ore coming out of his forehead, but on set that changed at a certain point and became a really vibrant blue with little lightning bolts and some other crazy stuff, which actually turned out even cooler.

The chin is another element from the original design. Joel said he thought it was part of his face and said, 'Run with it and see if it works,' so that's what I did. I don't usually get the chance to work that closely with the boss to figure it all out because I'm one of the new guys, so I wasn't expecting that.

I think that sculpture was originally done on a head cast of Ryan Reynolds. They had his head lying around from another show, so it was dropped on my desk and I said, 'Oh, is he in it?' and they said, 'No, no, you just need to work on this!' It was a really cool character to be part of.

CARLOS HUANTE: I know what all that stuff is when I draw, and exactly what I intended it to be, but the thing is some of those characters were used for something else so I didn't see the sculpts until I saw what they did with them in the film. This was an idea for the original bad guy, and that chin piece and the disc on his head were scarification things this character had that were supposed to be decorative. Those ideas were reused for the new character it became.

COCO

DESIGN AND SCULPT:

RICHIE ALONZO AND
JOEL HARLOW

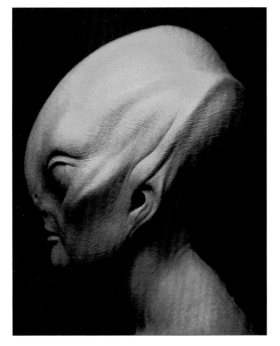

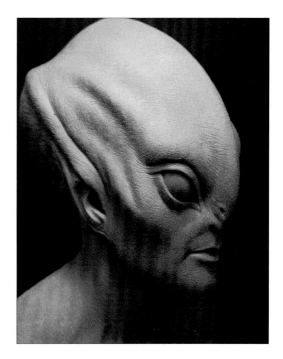

ABOVE: Originally based on the 'Madeline' character from the previous films, Coco eventually became a very different alien.

Y ou see one version of the character walking around the courtyard of Yorktown and another version at Kirk's birthday party with a different paint pattern. She started out when Richie Alonzo had begun re-sculpting the 'Madeline' character, which was an alien seen in the last two films. Madeline was a bronze-looking character with scarification tattoo markings, seen on the bridge of the *Enterprise*.

This sculpture, however, just didn't work on our actress's face. It didn't feel elegant; it just felt too long and awkward looking, so I changed it. Richie had already sculpted the back of the head beautifully, so I kept that element and changed its face and overall concept, spreading the eyes out and giving her four nostrils, but still making her look feminine. I added a bit of the classic gray alien to her, but as a makeup this time; something that could move, unlike what Don had done with the more mask-like version of our 'Classic Alien' character.

Another thing we did with this character in particular was paint vacuform domes for her eyes, so our actresses could see out through them. It was like looking out through very dark sunglasses, but since there's no light coming from inside you can't see that they're not completely opaque. She can see out, but when you look at her they just look like shiny black eyes. What that saved, of course, was having to animate a pupil looking around, because a black eye looking around is not going to show any movement at all. I believe when we see her at Kirk's birthday party they put a digital blink in her eyes, just to give her eyes a little bit of life.

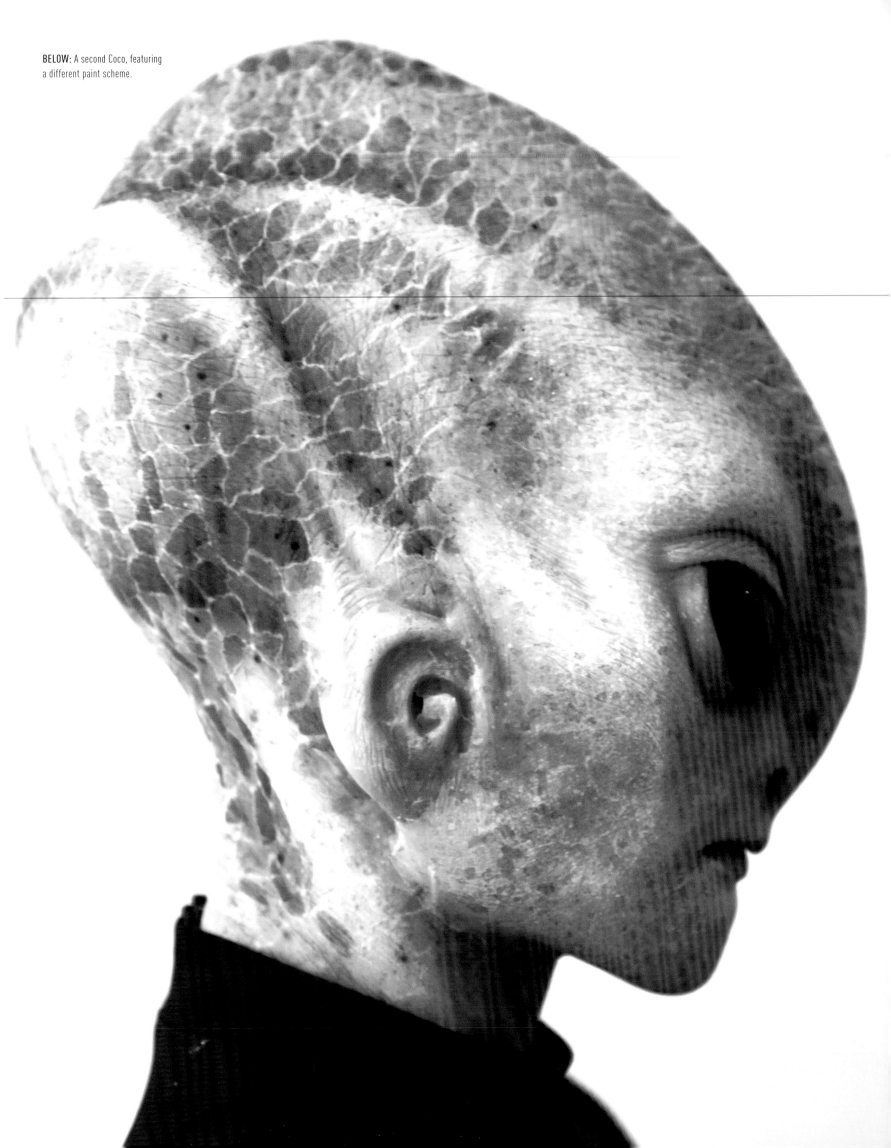

> "RICHIE HAD ALREADY SCULPTED THE BACK OF THE HEAD BEAUTIFULLY, SO I KEPT THAT ELEMENT AND CHANGED ITS FACE AND OVERALL CONCEPT."
>
> *Joel on Coco's evolution*

ABOVE: Black vacuform domes were used as eyes, with a digital blink added in post-production.

RICHIE ALONZO: That was actually a character that Neville Page had sculpted, who was the girl on the bridge in the first film. We started a new version of the sculpture because we knew they weren't going to bring the character back, but we said, 'Let's block it out and see what happens, because we could possibly use her for some other character!' I remember sculpting that character in the makeup trailer, and it became that alien. It also went through some changes, such as Joel saying, 'Let's give her artificial eyes,' so the original Madeline character eventually morphed into something else.

LOLEEKI

DESIGN: CARLOS HUANTE
SCULPT: LEE JOYNER

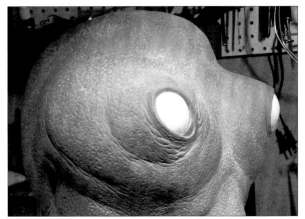

ABOVE: Lee Joyner's Loleeki sculpture before painting; an early Carlos Huante concept design that became Loleeki (below right).

This is another character designed by Carlos Huante as a background alien for the first pass of the script. Some of them didn't make it all the way through, but this one did because it was the favorite of a lot of the women in the production office, who thought it was cute.

I farmed the sculpture out to Lee Joyner, who couldn't join us in the shop. I still wanted him involved, so I sent a life cast and a pair of arm casts to him. He finished the sculptures for us out of his own studio. When he sent them back, we molded them and had Tim Ralston mechanize the head so its lips could pucker and its eyes could move independently of each other, kind of like a chameleon's eyes.

The really stellar part of this character is the amazing paint job done by Caitlin Groves. There are a couple of different versions of that paint scheme because we had two background masks and a mechanical foam head. When I saw it, it looked like a Photoshopped paint job because both sides were almost symmetrical. That really took the character to the next level for me. The sculpture lent itself to an ornate paint scheme because of its elegant simplicity. If you have a really intricate sculpture, you don't need an intricate paint job. Sometimes they work in opposition to each other, but when they work in unison, as they did with this character, it's pretty great.

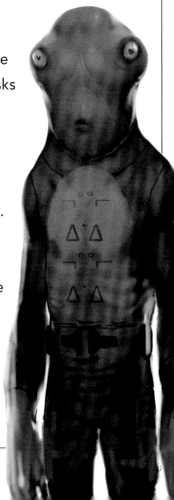

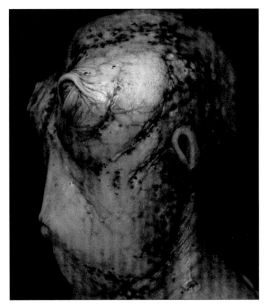

ABOVE: The Loleeki sculpture lent itself to an ornate paint scheme.

"THE SCULPTURE LENT ITSELF TO AN ORNATE PAINT SCHEME BECAUSE OF ITS ELEGANT SIMPLICITY. IF YOU HAVE A REALLY INTRICATE SCULPTURE, YOU DON'T NEED AN INTRICATE PAINT JOB."

Joel on the paint work done for Loleeki

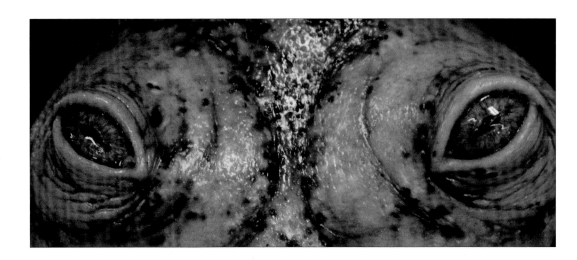

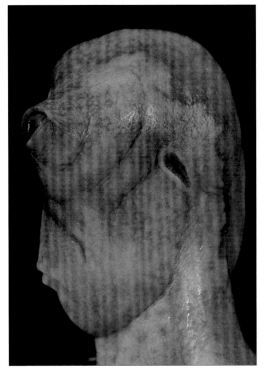
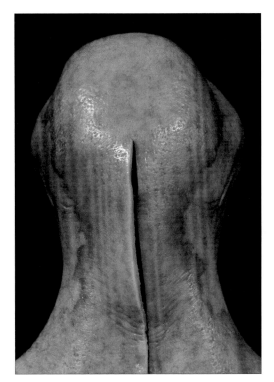
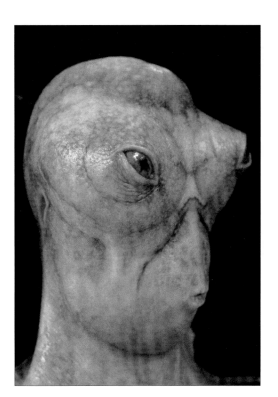

ABOVE: A second Loleeki, featuring a different, more restrained color palette.

BROK

DESIGN: CARLOS HUANTE
SCULPT: MATT ROSE

The character was designed by Carlos Huante as a background alien and the eyes, which I think are the most striking part of that makeup, were done by Rob Hinderstein. We glued that makeup on David Heffler, who was one of our makeup-effects coordinators. Lennie MacDonald spent a long time figuring out the mouth so that we could glue it down, so it wasn't a mask anymore and actually became a makeup. David Heffler's vision was very limited, but he worked around it and really sold the character.

Brok worked in Dubai, as did many of our background characters. A few of our prosthetics crew, myself included, needed to play some of the characters if we were going to get them into the film. We were all committed, however, about packing the screen with as many of our characters as possible.

LENNIE MACDONALD: I magnetized the eyes, so they could be popped out between scenes, and then I popped them back in when we started shooting. And because the eyes were magnetized, we could spin them if we needed the character to be looking one way or the other. The scary part was I had these beautiful Rob Hinderstein eyes and I had to actually drill into them in order to counter-synch the magnet. Those eyes were basically one-of-a-kind, so I had to make sure I didn't shatter the acrylic on them and that was a little nerve-racking!

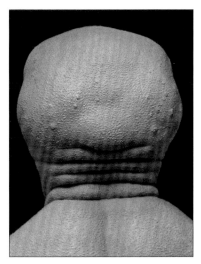
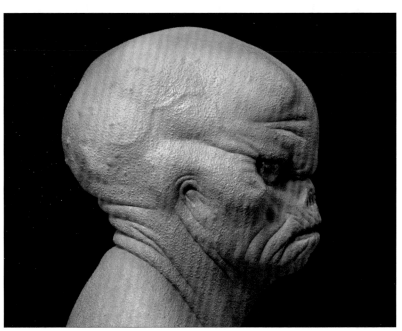

ABOVE: Different angles of Matt Rose's unpainted Brok sculpture.
RIGHT: This early Carlos Huante design for Brok shows how much a character can evolve over time.

CARLOS HUANTE: There were initially supposed to be three of those aliens; a father, a wife and son, and I think they did do something like that, so that was the idea with them. People don't really change that much; he still has two eyes, a nose and mouth, regardless of your color and maybe slight variations on the eyes, but they're still in the same place, so we don't really change that much as people between the various races.

"LENNIE MACDONALD SPENT A LONG TIME FIGURING OUT THE MOUTH SO THAT WE COULD GLUE IT DOWN, SO IT WASN'T A MASK ANYMORE AND ACTUALLY BECAME A MAKEUP."

Joel on nailing Brok's look

THIS PAGE: Two views of the painted Brok makeup before the addition of eyes.

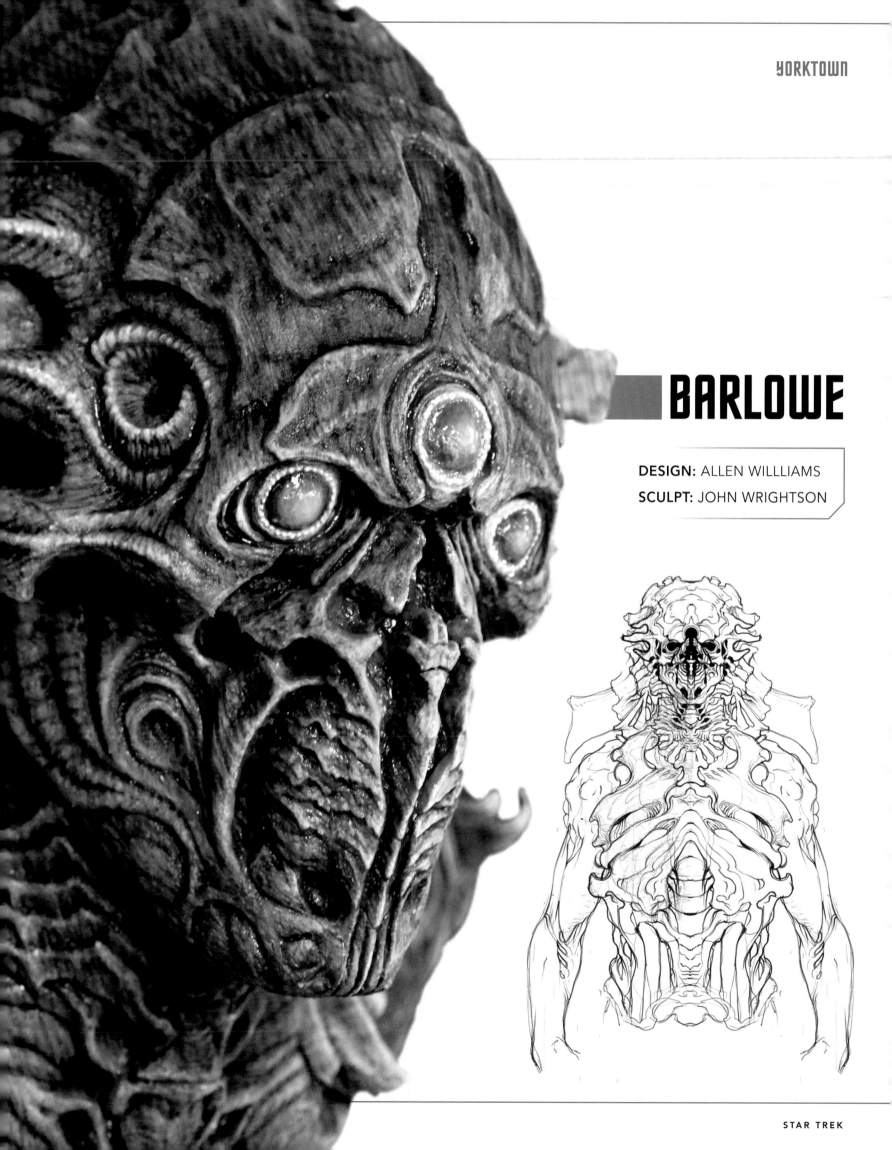

BARLOWE

DESIGN: ALLEN WILLLIAMS
SCULPT: JOHN WRIGHTSON

Even though the character came from an Allen Williams design, it felt like a Wayne Barlowe creature to me. That's why I named him Barlowe: it felt a bit demonic, like something out of the series of paintings from Wayne's book, *Inferno*.

ALLEN WILLIAMS: The fact that something I do might be reminiscent of Wayne Barlowe is no surprise to me because he's one of the people I really looked up to drawing-wise when learning how to draw, and how to draw in that particular style. I've actually worked with him on a few films, and he's a great guy to work around and just to observe his process. We both often work in graphite and we both finely render things, and we both have a way of putting together almost abstract shapes sometimes into a believable configuration. So it's happened quite a bit where people say, 'This reminds me of Barlowe!' and I'm flattered by that. When somebody says you remind them of somebody you've always looked up to, it's usually a good thing!

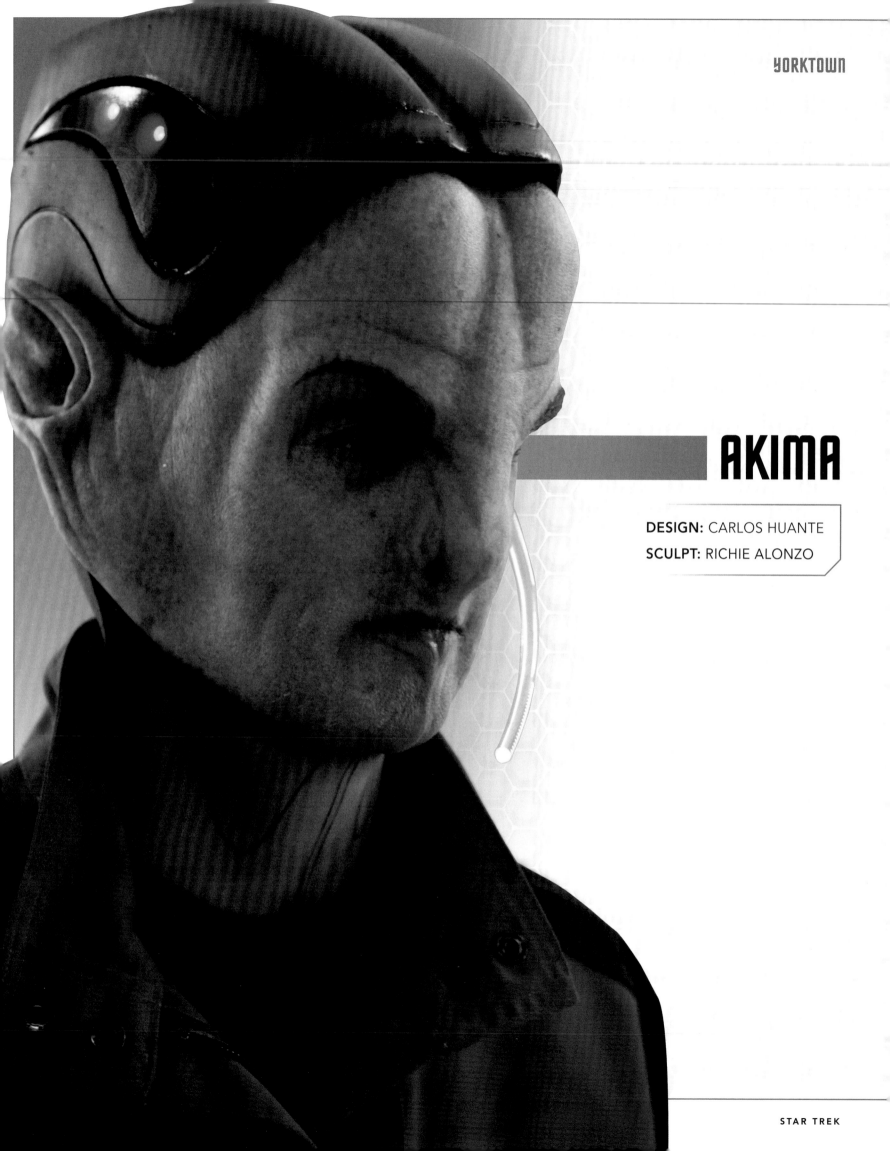

AKIMA

DESIGN: CARLOS HUANTE
SCULPT: RICHIE ALONZO

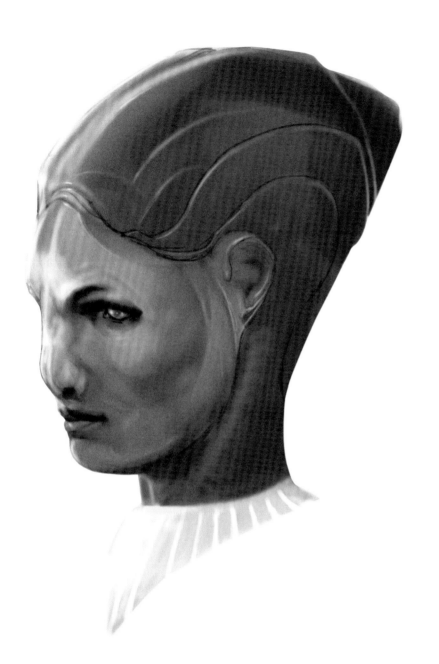

W e actually had two versions of the character: a Caucasian-skinned one with a glowing helmet, and a darker, African-skinned one with the grey helmet. We worked with the props department, who gave us a lit headset, and we removed a section from the helmet and replaced it with a set of glowing LEDs that would turn on and off. Adding that device made a nice breakup to the silhouette, so instead of just having a bald alien, this one had this weird futuristic headdress. It presented us with quite a molding challenge because the forehead came up so high. If you saw the character without its helmet it looked ridiculous because it's basically just a big bulb on top of the head. It doesn't really make sense until you put the helmet on that it all flows together.

My department built everything apart from the earpiece and the glowing LEDs. We did everything else, including the helmet and wardrobe neckpiece. The character had punched dark eyebrows for the light-skinned version and light eyebrows on the dark-skinned version. You don't get to see them very well in the film but you can see one of them when the *Enterprise* is docking; as Spock is coming out I believe she's behind him, next to the door to the *Enterprise*.

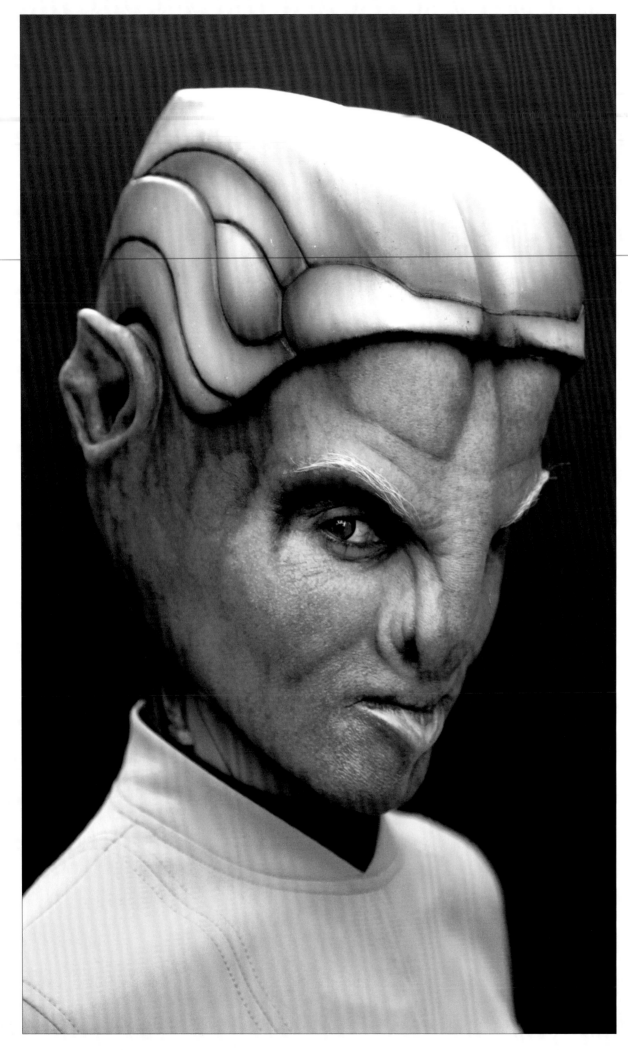

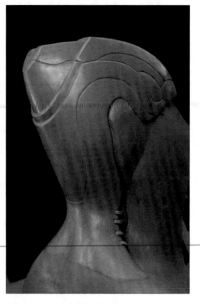

ABOVE: Unpainted Akima headpiece.

"IF YOU SAW THE
CHARACTER WITHOUT
ITS HELMET IT LOOKED
RIDICULOUS BECAUSE
IT'S BASICALLY JUST A
BIG BULB ON TOP OF THE
HEAD. IT DOESN'T REALLY
MAKE SENSE UNTIL
YOU PUT THE HELMET
ON THAT IT ALL FLOWS
TOGETHER."

Joel on Akima's distinctive headgear

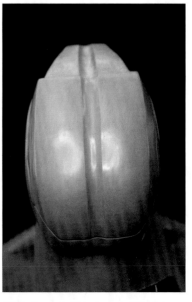

ABOVE: Top view of Akima's unpainted headpiece.

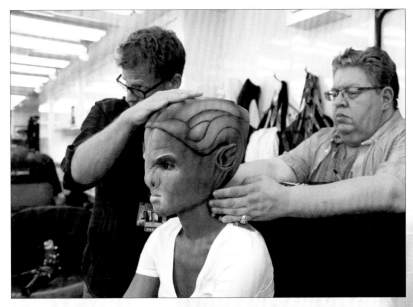

ABOVE: Joel Harlow and Richie Alonzo apply Akima makeup.

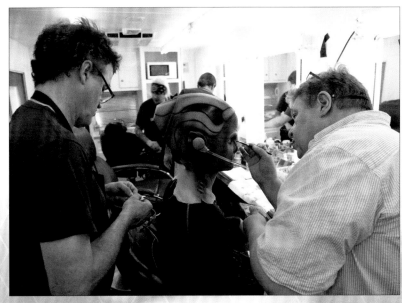

ABOVE: Lennie MacDonald adds electronic elements to Akima's headpiece while Alonzo touches up makeup.

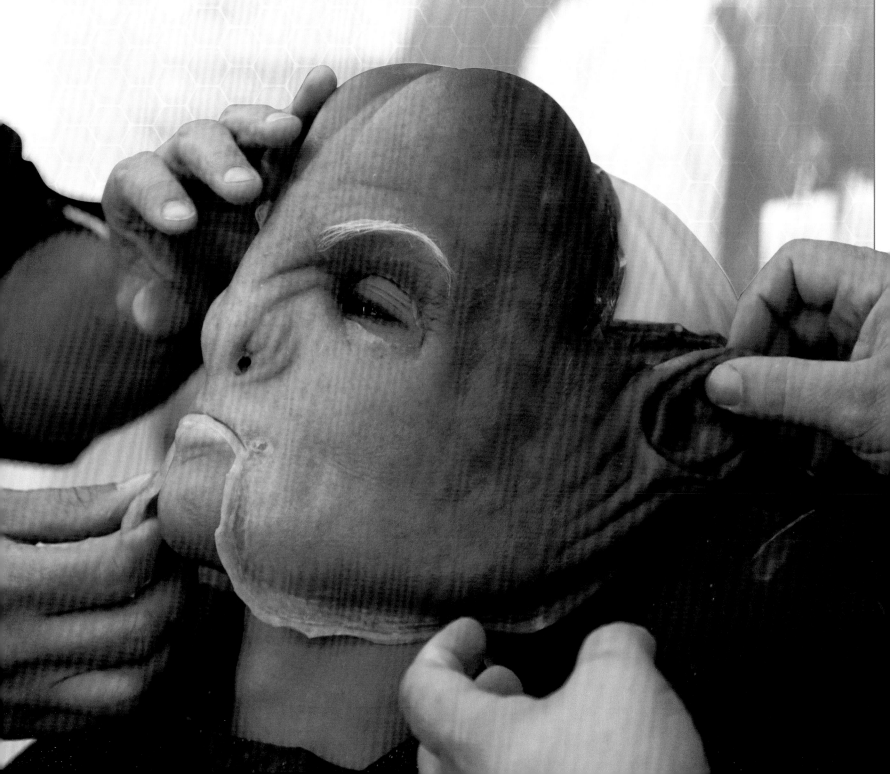

SNAIL

DESIGN: ALLEN WILLIAMS
SCULPT: JOHN WRIGHTSON

Snail was an Allen Williams design that John Wrightson sculpted. At one point we were going to mechanize the head, but there was no budget for it and it turned out that it really wasn't necessary. We already had a pair of hands that Mikey Rotella had sculpted when the Elephant Slug head was still the ambassador character, so we used those hands. We had Tim Ralston mechanize them, so those three long fingers would curl and bend like tentacles. I then gave them over to our amazing painters in Vancouver, who did some really interesting patterning on them.

You see the characters in the space dock where the *Enterprise* docks. Kirk comes out and I believe you see one quite well as it walks past him. All of our alien characters had at least two versions, and most of them had three. There are three versions of Loleeki, Snail, and Sheldon, and a couple versions of Shlerm. To fill out the scenes, we did multiples of a lot of our characters.

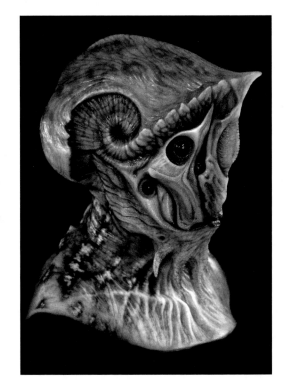

ABOVE: Three versions of Snail, each one featuring a different color palette.

JASKELL

DESIGN: JOEL HARLOW
SCULPT: RICHIE ALONZO

ABOVE: Jaskell is a hybrid character, comprised of prosthetic pieces from Jin, Shazeer and Coco.

We were at the very end of our shoot in Dubai when we discovered we needed one more alien. We didn't have the time or the crew to create a new character from scratch, but we had spare parts from over 50 characters and so it was pretty easy to piece something together based on what we already had with us. What you're looking at is a set of upside-down ears from Jin, Shazeer's face and the back of Coco's head.

Jaskell was the only alien we had to shortcut that way. Of course, none of the elements of this makeup were designed to fit together, so I was bridging the gaps between pieces with wedges of foam sponge. It actually turned out nicely, and ultimately it gets a pretty decent close-up when Kirk is getting thrown around in the slipstream during his fight with the more 'human' version of Krall at the end.

The Shazeer character, who became an alien control-tech character, was originally designed with a beard, but we ended up not using facial hair on the final version. Since the Jaskell character was the same sculpture, it seemed only natural to set it apart from Shazeer even further by giving him the unused beard. That's where his name comes from because he almost looks like a goat or a jackal, so 'Jaskell' felt like the right name for him when David Heffler (who played Jaskell) started referring to himself as that.

RICHIE ALONZO: Joel said, 'Okay, we're doing a new alien today. We're using this piece, that piece and those ears!' It included some ears I had sculpted, but sure enough it became another character and worked really well.

BEZOS

DESIGN AND SCULPT:
JOEL HARLOW

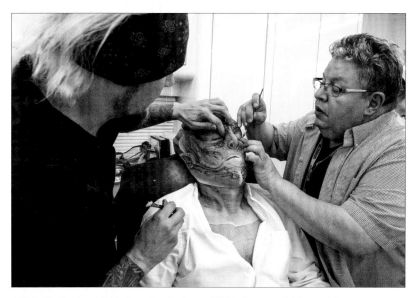
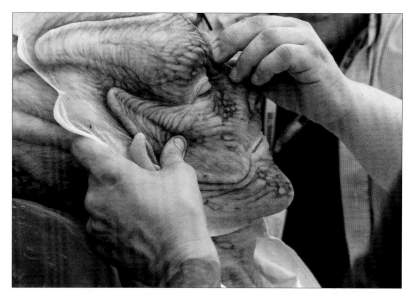

ABOVE: Mike Fields and Richie Alonzo turn the Amazon CEO into the appropriately named Bezos.

About halfway through filming I was approached by producer Lindsey Weber, who said Amazon CEO Jeff Bezos wanted to be a *Star Trek* alien. J.J. and Justin had already embraced the idea and wanted to put him in the film, so Lindsey asked if we had any generic aliens left that we could use for him. At that point we had pretty much used them all and I didn't want to rehash one of them on Jeff, so I sculpted a new one in the trailer during my lunch breaks and in between setups, specifically for him. I didn't have his life cast because we weren't going to get him until that day, so I sculpted the makeup generically. As it turned out, we were fortunate that it fit perfectly.

You actually see the character when Kalara is first taken into Yorktown as a refugee; he's the alien scanning her at the very beginning of the scene before she begins speaking through the translator. While Jeff didn't know exactly what he was getting into when he asked to be an alien, he was great in the chair. He really embraced it, and I think he even posted a video online as that alien character while he was having lunch and you could tell he was happy.

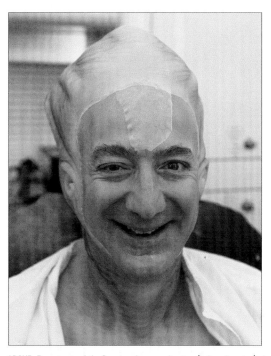

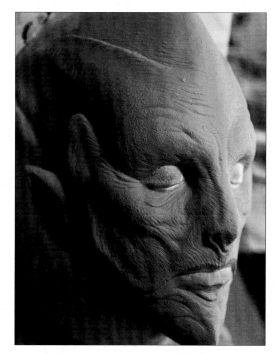

ABOVE: Two stages of the Bezos makeup application (left and center); Joel Harlow's original Bezos sculpture (right).

RUSS

DESIGN: NEVILLE PAGE

SCULPT: NORMAN CABRERA, DON LANNING (HANDS)

ABOVE: (From left to right): Unpainted and painted Russ; the finished character in wardrobe; another angle of the painted version.

Russ is the character you see with the Elephant Slug—he's his owner. He was a Neville Page design and Norman Cabrera sculpture. Don Lanning sculpted the hands, which were repurposed hands from the Quills character, mechanized by Tim Ralston. They were quite large, so they had a slave system inside with rings that went onto the actor's fingers so when he moved his fingers, the fingers of the creature would move. We added mechanics in the head to give him some expression, as well as some mouth articulation. I believe we made three of those characters, only one of which was mechanized. There are some flaps in the front of it and a lower lip that were all separately hinged so they could move in a very alien fashion.

ABOVE: The Russ hands were sculpted by Don Lanning and mechanized by Tim Ralston (jewelry sold separately!)

BOGGS

DESIGN AND SCULPT:
DON LANNING

ABOVE: (From left to right): Unpainted Boggs; Don Lanning works on his Boggs sculpture; the finished character.

Boggs was one of the very first characters we built. Don Lanning did an initial maquette, and then we made three full-sized versions. We wanted some movement out of the masks, so I had Tim Ralston give them simple points of movement. There was one 'hero' Boggs that could move its mouth and move its eyes around, and the other two were background masks. That completed the race. I guess 'Boggs' would be a race name as opposed to an individual proper alien name. You see the hero Boggs in Yorktown, where the *Enterprise* docks, in the same area as Akima. You also see them in the courtyard exteriors on Yorktown.

ABOVE: Three different versions of the 'Boggs' race.

DON LANNING: I was giving Joel two maquettes a day, and at that point he was letting me work in my own studio in Sherman Oaks. Some of the designs got pretty wacky, and knowing that some of these heads were going to be in deep background, we went for some bizarre head shapes, so that was the mandate with this character. I was also thinking about trees that lose their bark, so that was part of the inspiration.

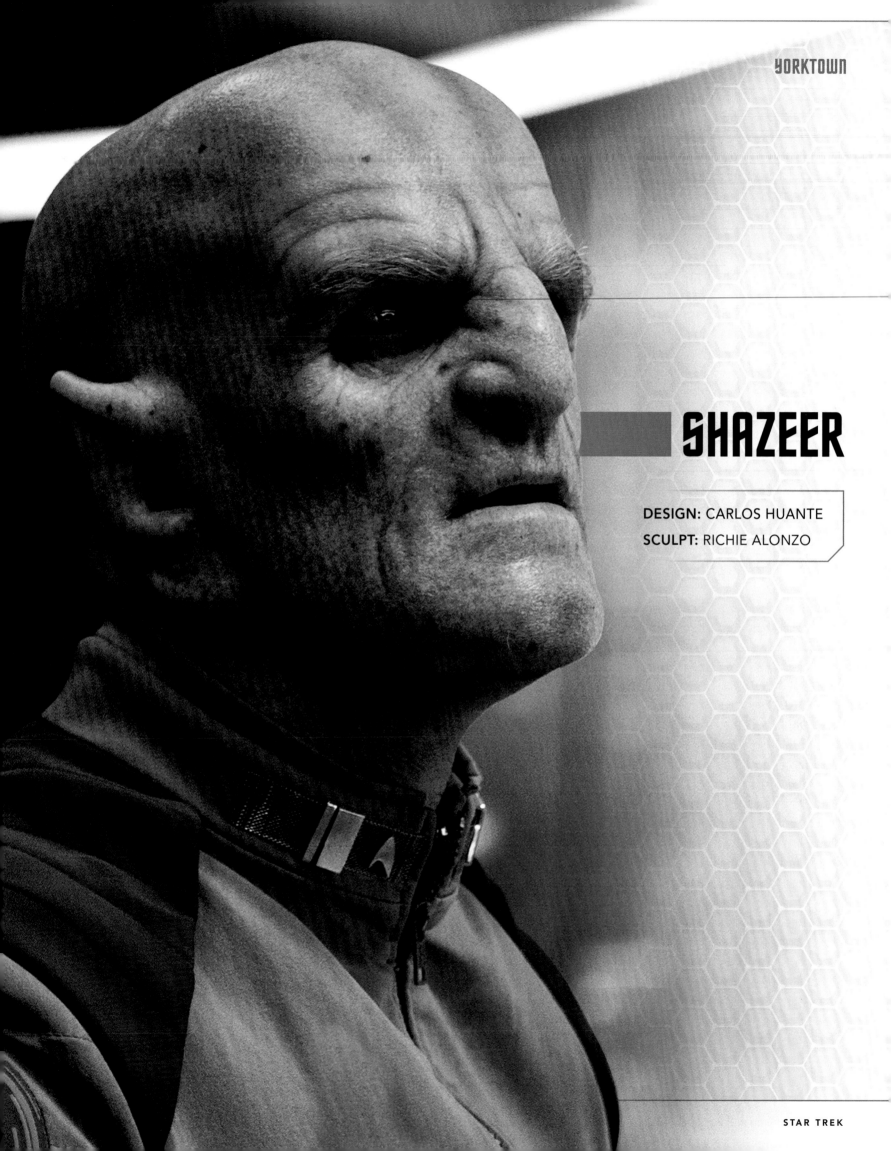

SHAZEER

DESIGN: CARLOS HUANTE
SCULPT: RICHIE ALONZO

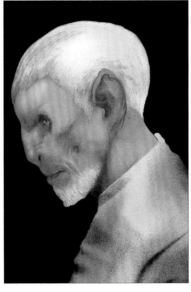

ABOVE: (From left to right): Richie Alonzo's Shazeer sculpture; the early Carlos Huante concept design; the finished character.

This character became pretty important actually. There was an alien at the beginning of *Star Trek Into Darkness* that was played by a gentleman named Jeremy Raymond. Jeremy jumped on board to play another alien character in our film. He's in the control-tech center when Kalara's ship comes in, and they wanted the character to have some dialogue. We ended up going with the Shazeer makeup design (which was renamed 'control-tech alien' in the credits) for him because it allowed for quite a bit of expression.

The makeup fit him great, which is always the worry when you upgrade a generic character to a hero makeup: if the pieces don't fit exactly right and they've got dialogue, you're really going to notice it.

ABOVE: Joel Harlow applies the Shazeer makeup.

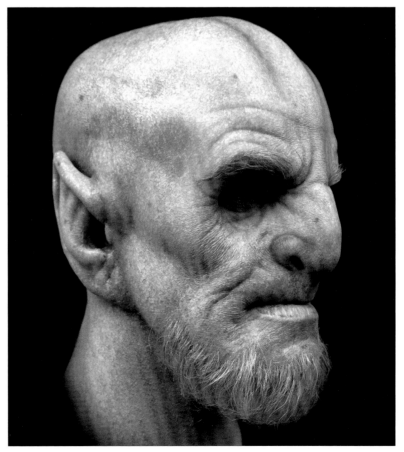

ABOVE: An earlier bearded version of character.

THROG

DESIGN: NEVILLE PAGE
SCULPT: MATT ROSE

  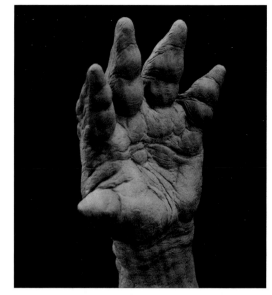

ABOVE: (From left to right): The Throg sculpture; the painted version; a close-up of one of Throg's hands.

uring an early version of the script when the elephant slug-headed alien was still being designed as an ambassador character, it was scripted that there were going to be two of these Throg characters flanking the ambassador on the left and right—they were his security detail. At the point when that part of the prologue went away, Matt Rose had already beautifully sculpted the Throg character's head, so we knew we

were determined to get it in a scene somewhere. We were initially going to mechanize the head, but, like a few of the other larger-headed alien characters, we ran out of time and money.

We made two of them and painted them very differently. You can see one of them in the same place as many of our big-headed aliens, which is the Starfleet dock interior.

ABOVE: Matt Rose works on the Throg sculpture.

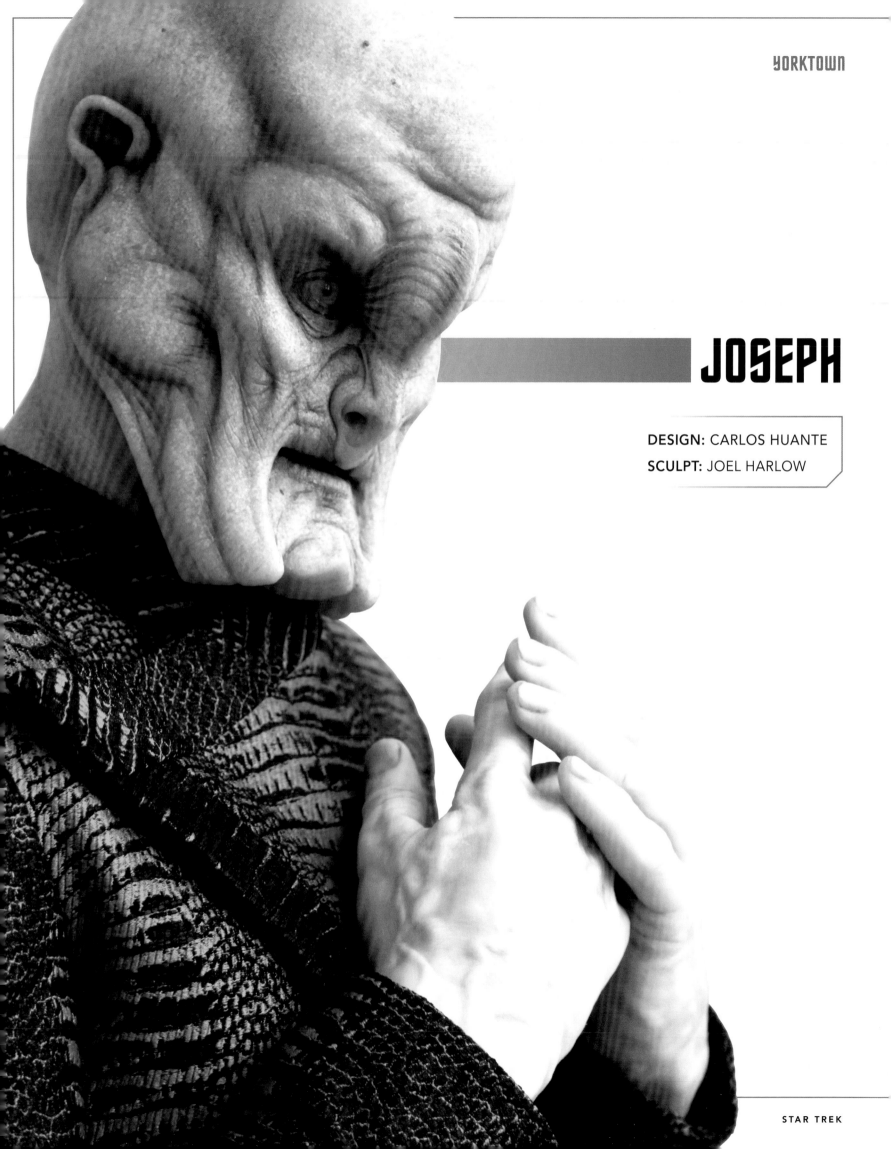

JOSEPH

DESIGN: CARLOS HUANTE
SCULPT: JOEL HARLOW

This was a design Carlos Huante had done at the beginning when we had a different script, so that was a holdover like Boltaan and Shazeer. I thought the design, which reminded me of a beluga whale, was very exciting, and since we needed to start populating our world I jumped on that one. The name came from the size and shape of the character's head, because he reminded me of Joseph Merrick, the Elephant Man. This was the first sculpture I did for the film.

We also used the trick I had mentioned earlier with reference to Crabbie, that Barney Burman used in the first *Star Trek* film, which involves taking a life cast of someone's hands, pouring them out of silicone and putting them in kerosene so they swell. Once you mold them and core the molds out, you've got a giant, hyper-detailed human hand that can become a glove. That's what we did with Joseph to keep his hands in proportion with his large head.

ABOVE: Harlow working on the Joseph sculpture.

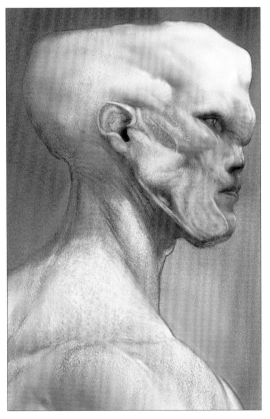  

ABOVE: The evolution of Joseph from Carlos Huante's initial design, to Joel Harlow's sculpture, to the finished character.

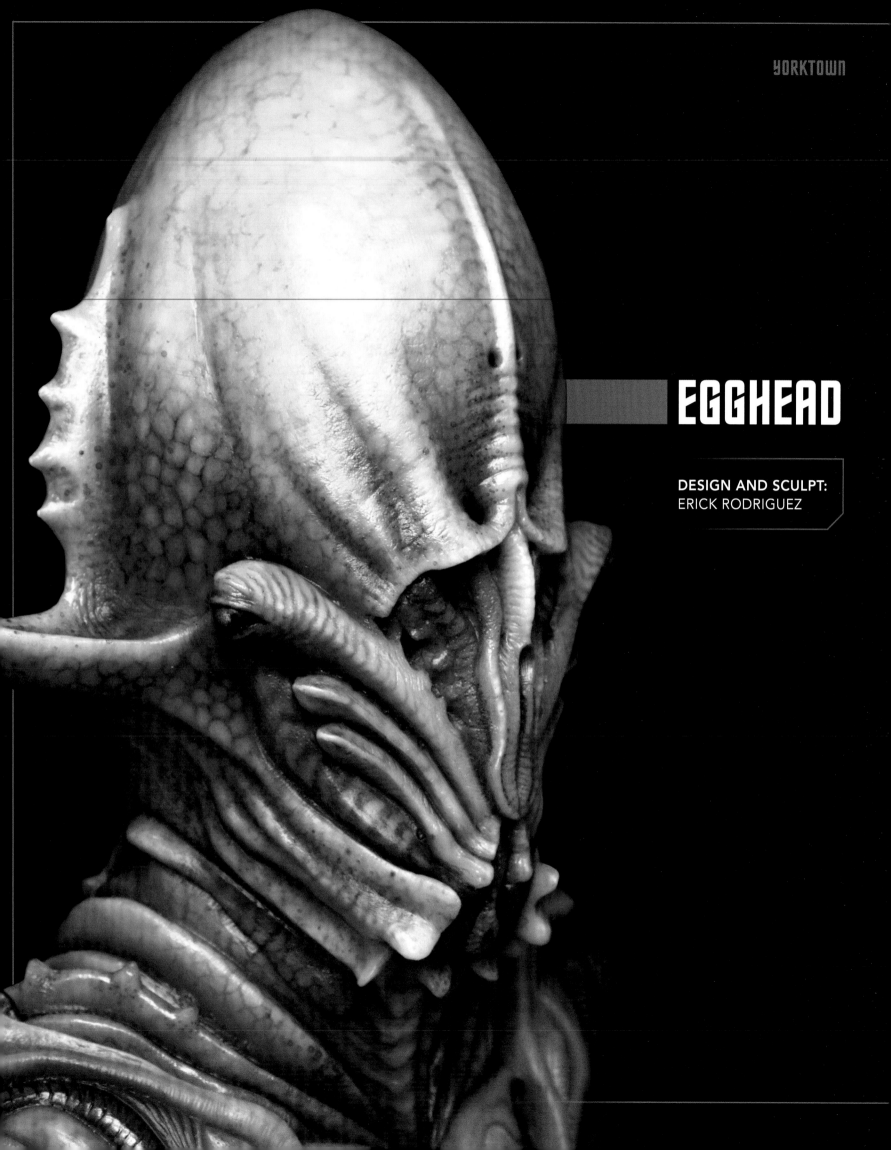

EGGHEAD

DESIGN AND SCULPT:
ERICK RODRIGUEZ

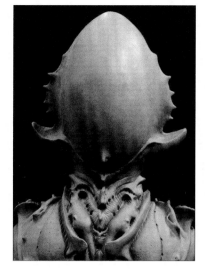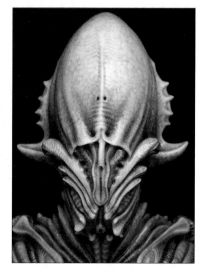

ABOVE: Unfinished and painted versions of the Egghead character.

I met Erick Rodriguez during the time that we had a huge influx of needed characters. We needed to get these characters translated into sculptures and then molds before we headed up to Vancouver. I ran into Erick at the Son of Monsterpalooza show and he had this brilliant-looking alien maquette sitting on his table, so I asked him if he wanted to come and work on *Star Trek*, and of course he did. When he came on board I said, 'Why don't you translate that character of yours from the show, and turn it into a background mask?' so that's what he did. The striking blue paint scheme was done by one of my Vancouver artists, which really pushed it to the next level. Erick also sculpted and designed the hands for this character.

Three of these aliens appear in the movie at the space dock in Yorktown. Sanja Hays provided an excellent compliment to the aesthetic with a series of blue robes. We had deliberately cast tall actors to play the characters, and Sanja also gave them lifts to push their height even further. The lifts, combined with the height of their heads, brought them up to an impressive 7'6"–8' in height.

ABOVE: Steve Buscaino oversees the application of Egghead's arms; front and side views of the finished head.

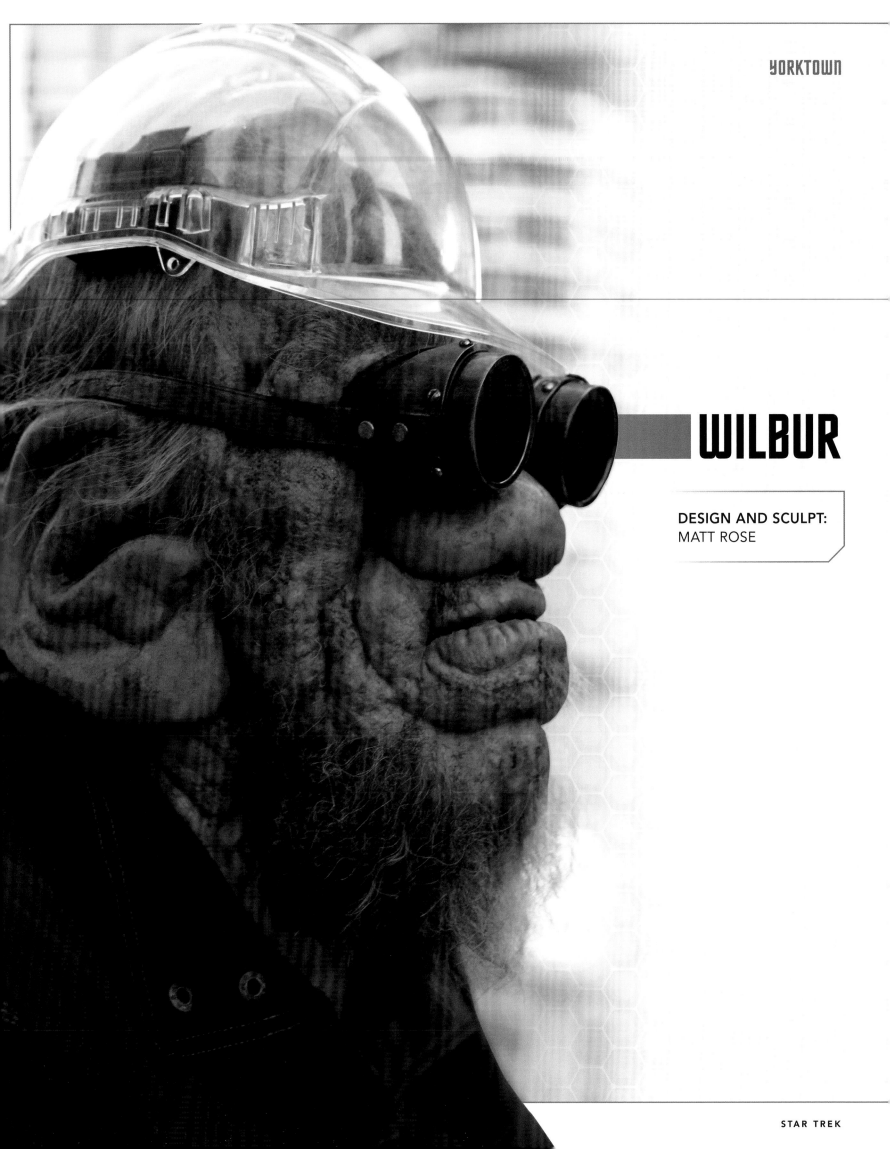

WILBUR

DESIGN AND SCULPT:
MATT ROSE

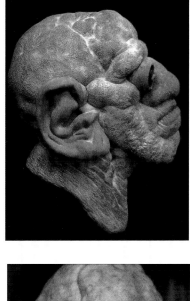

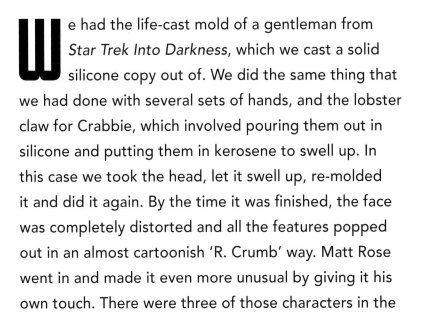

ABOVE: The 'Wilburs' became the janitors of Yorktown.

ABOVE: Different paint scheme turns one Wilbur into two.

We had the life-cast mold of a gentleman from *Star Trek Into Darkness*, which we cast a solid silicone copy out of. We did the same thing that we had done with several sets of hands, and the lobster claw for Crabbie, which involved pouring them out in silicone and putting them in kerosene to swell up. In this case we took the head, let it swell up, re-molded it and did it again. By the time it was finished, the face was completely distorted and all the features popped out in an almost cartoonish 'R. Crumb' way. Matt Rose went in and made it even more unusual by giving it his own touch. There were three of those characters in the Yorktown courtyard exterior; they're almost a cleanup crew, so Sanja dressed them in high-tech janitor outfits.

There really was no design for the Wilbur characters; once I saw how successful it was using kerosene to swell the silicone hands we turned into gloves for Boltaan and Joseph, I wanted to see what it would do to a head. Once the features get hyper-distorted, all the wrinkles, crevices and separations between the features get even deeper. Because they were masks, and we didn't want to limit the vision of the performers that would be wearing them, we decided to add the bug-eyed goggles, which work very nicely with the overall look.

MATT ROSE: This guy had an incredible face to begin with, and then they swelled it up once and Joel said, 'Put it back in and swell it up again!' so we ended up with this huge mask, which I was given to retouch. I also gave him bigger ears, so it was really interesting the way that character turned out.

PESCA

DESIGN: JOEL HARLOW

SCULPT: JOEL HARLOW
AND JOHN WRIGHTSON

originally started the sculpture on this character, but I ran out of time because we were packing up for Vancouver so I passed it on to John Wrightson to finish off, and he did a great job. This character is another makeup that I did on my stepdaughter, Ashley. We filmed her in Dubai and since Ashley was already there anyway to play the part of Natalia, it was an easy decision to put her in the Pesca makeup as well, especially as it was in a completely different scene shot on a different day.

This character has a lot of that color-shifting pigment in it that Lennie MacDonald sourced and engineered. She's a teacher so you see her at Yorktown in the courtyard, surrounded by the children she's teaching.

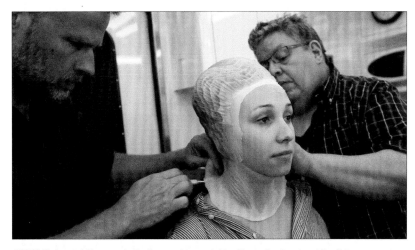

ABOVE: Harlow and Alonzo apply the Pesca makeup to Ashley Edner, who also played Natalia.

ALA

DESIGN AND SCULPT: JOEL HARLOW

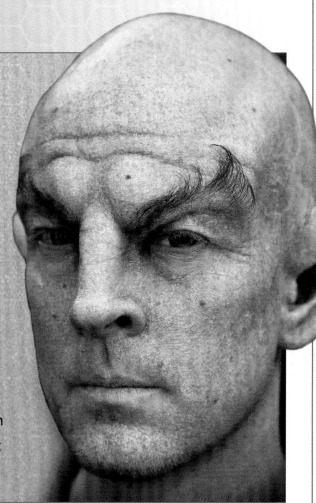

What ALA actually stands for is 'Awesome Little Alien,' and it refers to a bald, yellow-skinned character we created. It basically has a Romulan forehead from the first film and a pair of ears, and that's pretty much it. We needed to add another alien for the control tech scene when Kalara shows up at Yorktown in her ship. I don't think you see him in the final film, but we were trying to populate that control tech area with more aliens, which is why this one was created.

There was actually another makeup I had done on one of the coordinators that was so awful that it never saw the light of day, so we referred to it as 'SLA' which is 'S**tty Little Alien'. So when we did this one I thought, 'I'll just call him ALA!' I don't think I even took any photos of the SLA. On a film like this, you end up testing a lot of different ideas. Sometimes they work well, and other times they blow up in your face. On *Star Trek Beyond* I think everything else was ALA, and I was happy to put all of them in front of the camera.

CHAPTER 5

CLOSING THOUGHTS

The Oscar race was very different on this film than it was on the first *Star Trek*. Whereas I did very little publicity on that film, I really did most of the campaigning on this one; not so much to win (because you never really know what's going to happen), but just to get the word out on what we had done. Once your film goes to the Academy, you generally don't know what criteria people are going to vote on, or what criteria they should be voting on. You can't predict anything. That's why they say once you get to the final three nominated films, which are chosen by your peers, everybody is a winner. I think that's absolutely true because the 'makeup artists and hairstylists' branch picks those films based on the criteria that our category should be judged upon.

I will admit it was disappointing not to win this time because the work we accomplished on this film, the variety, the complexity, the quantity and the quality, is very rare. It only happened because of the crew I was working with, so it would have been a real win for the crew. As far as publicity went, I was very adamant about acknowledging our crew when speaking about everything we did, so when we didn't win it was a blow because who knows, this might turn out to be my last *Star Trek* film. You never know about these things, but coming as far as we did with design and character creation and going so over-the-top for the fans with some of our characters and for ourselves (who are also fans) it was a blow, but it doesn't diminish one bit the work we did together.

I would do another *Star Trek* film in a heartbeat, and hope that I have that opportunity. We did hundreds and hundreds of designs for this one, so there's still a wealth of material that deserves three-dimensional expression. If another sequel happens, I would hope I could get the same crew, and maybe even some additional folks I've met along the way who I think would be valuable additions to the team. It is my passion to create interesting characters and to be artistic; this film afforded me that opportunity to the millionth degree. That's why I got into this business and it's more valuable than any award.

I do feel the need to speak about the crew once more. The work you have just seen in this book would not have been possible without every single one of them. Remove a single crew person and the art would have undoubtedly suffered. This isn't always the standard. Egos and ambition can easily taint the process. I have worked with many crews over the course of my career, some as captain, some as crewman, and I can tell you these individuals absolutely shined. It isn't always easy to lead a band of artists… especially those you respect and admire.

From the inception of our designs, sculptures, and lab work in Burbank, to the casting, paintwork, and finishing in Vancouver, they all made it easy for me to do my job by being enthusiastic, artistically brilliant, professional, and completely supportive. My heartfelt thanks goes out to all of them and I would gladly go 'Beyond' with them any day.

LEFT: The Vancouver team at the end of production.
1. Gil Liberto; 2. Tegan Colby; 3. Richie Alonzo;
4. Bryan Blair; 5. Lance Webb; 6. Shelagh McIvor;
7. Crissy Renaud; 8. Joel Harlow; 9. Cindy Harlow;
10. Corinne De Berry; 11. Caitlin Groves; 12. Felix Fox;
13. Lennie MacDonald; 14. Steve Buscaino;
15. Daemon Cadman; 16. Bronwyn Sloley;
17. Kyle Huculak; 18. Jeff LeBlanc; 19. Brittney Bolzan;
20. Carolyn Williams; 21. Matthew Aebig;
22. Erin Peters; 23. Jen Machnee; 24. Pearl Louie;
25. Holland Miller; 26. Kalynn Kallweit

LEFT: The Burbank team. 1. Joey Orosco;
2. Taylor MacDonald; 3. Charlie Trent;
4. Lennie MacDonald; 5. Mike Rotella;
6. Josh Sacks; 7. Norman Cabrera; 8. Harry Blom;
9. Chris Evitt; 10. Miles Teves; 11. John Wrightson;
12. Jocelyn Alcazar; 13. Johnny Saiko;
14. Bobby Edner; 15. Scott Fields; 16. Gil Liberto;
17. Todd Bates; 18. Pedro Valdez; 19. Khanh Trace;
20. Wilson Pollak; 21. Josh McCarron;
22. Joel Harlow; 23. Chris Baer; 24. Don Lanning;
25. Cindy Harlow; 26. Bryan Blair; 27. John Halfman;
28. Matt Rose; 29. Steve Buscaino; 30. Alex Noble;
31. Richie Alonzo

LEFT: The Dubai team. 1. Lennie MacDonald;
2. Tracy Lai; 3. Steve Buscaino; 4. Cindy Harlow;
5. Michael Fields; 6. Joel Harlow; 7. Bryan Blair;
8. Debra Szteina; 9. Gil Liberto; 10. Jenny Irons;
11. Richie Alonzo; 12. Felix Fox; 13. Werner Pretorius;
14. David Heffler

BELOW: The Vancouver team at the start of production. 1. Steve Buscaino; 2. Bronwyn Sloley; 3. Carolyn Williams; 4. Toby Lindala; 5. Lennie MacDonald; 6. Lance Webb; 7. Bryan Blair; 8. Joey Orosco; 9. Cindy Harlow; 10. Joel Harlow; 11. Raj Mairathasan; 12. Khanh Trace; 13. Nicholas Podbry; 14. David Heffler; 15. Shelagh McIvor; 16. Caitlin Groves; 17. Amelia Smart; 18. Corinne De Berry; 19. Tegan Colby; 20. Frida Norrman; 21. Matthew Aebig; 22. Tracy Lai; 23. Jeff LeBlanc; 24. Gil Liberto; 25. Werner Pretorius; 26. Gideon Hay; 27. Erin Peters; 28. Richie Alonzo; 29. John Halfman

RICHIE ALONZO: The awards season was physically taxing because we were working in Atlanta and traveling to L.A. almost every weekend, so you would work 15–16 -hour days all week and hop on a red-eye to L.A. on Friday night and go to IMATS or a makeup symposium and finally the Oscars, which I was really looking forward to, but all of it was kind of overwhelming.

I flew in my sister from Charlotte, North Carolina to come with me to the Oscars, so I had to handle her flight and make sure she was okay getting to the airport, so there was just so much on my plate; getting emails from the Academy and the Makeup Symposium and going to the Oscar luncheon, which was great, so there was so much happening on a weekly basis and it was kind of taxing, trying to muster the energy that's needed, so I would try and close my eyes and take a little nap whenever I could, especially on the plane. I really relished that time to just close my eyes and forget about everything until I landed.

But the whole thing was really exciting, and I have to thank Joel for creating that opportunity for me and making all that happen. He was a great department head and a great boss to work for, even though he doesn't like to be called the boss. Joel just likes to give you a character and say, 'Here, make this happen!' and so he gives you the creative freedom you need. We would get input from the production and the producers and director as to what they wanted to see, but Joel always managed to steer the ship. He had the confidence in knowing he had people who could do the job, and felt confident we could do it and that everything would look good, so it was a great opportunity.

In the beginning, I didn't know Jaylah was going to become such a big character in the *Star Trek* world, so the pressure was really on. She had to be attractive and she had to look cool and become this character everyone would gravitate toward, and happily it's turned out that way. I'm shocked by all the YouTube videos that you see,

especially with these young girls who are enamored with this character. She's this really cool female alien character in the *Star Trek* universe, and now they're going through these extreme lengths to mimic and copy her makeup, and attempting to do it themselves. You've got to give these people tremendous credit because it's not easy, but they're trying their best and the results are amazing in terms of how they've been able to create their own Jaylah makeup.

I guess it says a lot in the sense that they really liked the character, so for me that's very satisfying, that it's a character I was able to work on that has become a staple in the *Star Trek* universe, along with the Andorians and other alien races we've seen in the various *Star Trek* TV shows and films.

DON LANNING: *Star Trek* has been with me my whole life, so just to have the privilege to work on it with great people with a progressive agenda artistically—and the

ability to get it done and to get it done with high art direction—was a highlight. I made some real friendships on *Star Trek Beyond* and I've got to say for me the experience is going to be remembered as an intensely artistic time of high productivity.

But also, and I mentioned this to Joel, at a certain point when we had the sculpting crew in Burbank assembled and the room went from an empty room within a couple of weeks to being filled with sculptors giving their best to realize their individual characters, the room became incredibly artistic and there was a tremendous amount of experience on the show. So you had the journeymen doing their thing, and you have the newer guys like John Wrightson and Mikey Rotella stepping up to the plate and doing some amazing work, so they were in there swinging as hard as they could.

But my favorite memory was getting a call from your buddy and saying, 'Hey, we've got *Star Trek*; let's go to work!' You can't ask for more than that!

AFTERWORD

BY SOFIA BOUTELLA

When I arrived at the Paramount Studio lot in Los Angeles in early 2015 for a call-back audition, I knew little of what was in store, only that the role related to *Star Trek*. The script was shrouded in secrecy and there were few details about the character or the story. My only instruction was to arrive with no makeup on my face, not even moisturizer.

As I made my way inside I was greeted by director Justin Lin, who sat me down and gave me more information about the character and how the creative team envisioned her appearance. I was told that this would be more of a screen test than an audition and was ushered into a large makeup trailer. Tools of all shapes and sizes were spread out before me and each makeup artist wore an apron; this was clearly a serious operation! The room buzzed with energy and enthusiasm as preparations were made. It was at this point that I met the captain of the ship, Joel Harlow. With a giant smile on his face he introduced himself and asked, "Do you know what you're going to look like?" "No," I replied, "I don't even know if I have the part." "You will", he said with confidence. He proceeded to show me a beautiful and perfectly sculpted bust of Jaylah. I was amazed, nervous even, to think that I would soon be transformed into this extraordinary character, but I surrendered myself to Joel, Richie Alonzo, and the team of amazing artists.

I quickly became fascinated and intrigued by the fine details of their handiwork. In the three hours it took to apply the design, I witnessed Joel in his element, blending childlike imagination with mature observation to every detail of Jaylah's beguiling face. Using a variety of paints and airbrush tools I had never seen before, Jaylah slowly but surely came into view. When I finally looked into her feline eyes for the first time, I swear there was no mirror between us. It was a face I have come to know very well.

I was so humbled to be given the opportunity to play Jaylah, and thrilled to be able to realise the character so completely, aided by such a flawlessly realistic appearance. Actors constantly transform emotionally, but rarely get the chance to physically transform to this extent. Thanks to Joel's skill, imagination and artistic precision, I was given that opportunity and it was an experience I shall never forget.

Joel's work has left an indelible mark on the landscape of film, but also on those lucky enough to see his work in action. The monsters, the aliens, the zombies, the pirates and the humans that spring from his imagination give those actors behind the makeup the tools to create truly memorable characterisations and bring heartfelt life to the unlikeliest of faces. It is an honor to be a part of such a meaningful and intelligent legacy. One that has mixed wild imagination, gripping entertainment and a defiance of social expectation. These attributes define Joel Harlow's work, and I will forever be amazed and inspired by the passion, talent and dedication he applies to his craft.

SOFIA BOUTELLA

ACKNOWLEDGMENTS

This book began life way back in the spring of 2016. Joel Harlow and I had just done an extensive interview about *Star Trek Beyond* for Neill Gorton's wonderful *Prosthetics* magazine, and after looking at a PDF of some 200-odd photos that Joel had sent Paramount publicity for clearance, I asked how many more images he might have in his possession. 'Thousands' was the answer, at which point I suggested there might be enough material for an entire book. A few months later, I had dinner in London with Nick Landau and Vivian Cheung from Titan Books, and we were off and running.

I would like to thank Nick and Vivian for taking my word that we definitely had more than enough images to put together an amazing-looking book while only seeing a small handful to start with. Thanks also to editor Andy Jones, who inherited the project after it was already in the works but immediately made it his own. And much praise has to go to the Titan art department, who have had to slog through more alien images than anybody should ever have to look at. Not only that, they've taken the best of those images and turned them into an amazingly beautiful piece of work.

Big thanks to the team at *Star Trek Beyond*—not only the folks who were so generous with their time, but everybody from painters to mold-makers to contact-lens technicians, whose collective DNA permeates every page of this book.

I reserve my biggest thanks to Joel Harlow, who put up with my endless questions, comments and requests, all while shooting two other films back to back. I'm not quite sure Joel had any idea what would happen when he agreed that yes, there was plenty of material for a book. As the saying goes, be careful what you wish for...

Joe Nazzaro, March 2017

THE STAR TREK BEYOND TEAM

Designer/Head of Department:
Joel Harlow

Sculptors: Joey Orosco, Matt Rose, Richie Alonzo, Don Lanning, Norman Cabrera, Miles Teves, Marc Opdycke, Erick Rodriguez, Mike Rotella, Lee Joyner, John Wrightson

Designers: Carlos Huante, Allen Williams, Neville Page, Joe Pepe

Painters: Lance Webb, Bronwyne Sloley, Erin Peters, Caitlin Groves, Daemon Cadman

Lab Supervisor: Steve Buscaino

Mold Supervisor: Gil Liberto

Hair Fabrication:
Khanh Trace, Lynn Watson

Lab: Alex Noble, Charlie Trent, Josh McCarron, Pedro Valdez, Todd Bates, Bryan Blair, Scott Fields, Harry Blom, Chris Baer, John Halfman, AJ Venuto, Matthew Aebig, Brittany Bolzan, Daemon Cadman, Tegan Colby, Kyle Huculak, Tracy Lai, Jeff LeBlanc, Raj Mairathasan, Frida Norrman, Amelia Smart, Corinne De Berry, David Mosher, Johnny Saiko, Wilson Pollak, Carolyn Williams, Josh Sacks, Erin Peters, Kalynn Kallweit, Jen Machnee, Gideon Hay, Brittney Bolzan

Eyes: Marcine Peter, Debra Szteina, Rob Hinderstein, Cristina Patterson, Bob Smithson

Mechanics: Tim Ralston

Foam: Rolland Blancaflor

Administrative: Cindy Harlow, Chris Evitt, David Heffler, Bobby Edner, Jenny Irons

Makeup Artists: Richie Alonzo, Lennie MacDonald, Werner Pretorius, Michael Fields, Felix Fox, Kevin Haney, Toby Lindala, Harlowe MacFarlane, Kenny Myers, Shelagh McIvor, Brad Look, Monica Huppert, Charles Porlier, Suzie Klimack, Ed French, Geoff Rednap, Sarah Graham, Maiko 'Mo' Gomyo, Patricia Murray, Holland Miller, Margaret Prentice, Darah Wyant, Jennifer Machnee, Rebecca Delchambre, Megan Harkness, Zera Azmi

Hair Department: Anne Carroll, Karen Myers, Robert Pandini, Barbara Cantu, Alisa Macmillan, Thom MacIntyre

Cleanup: Darah Wyant, Jen Machnee, Pearl Louie

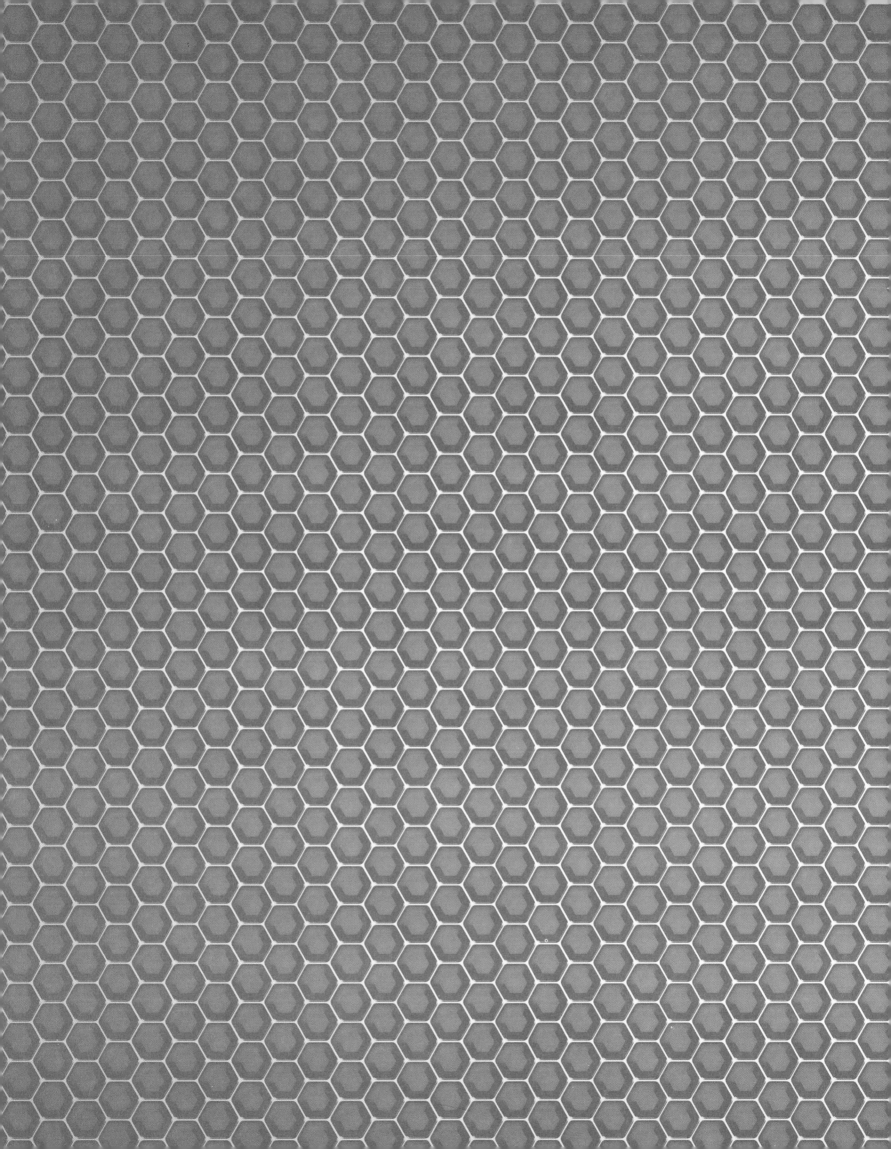